WOUND
MANAGEMENT
GUIDE

PROUDLY NZ OWNED.

USL has been built by creating seamless relationships. Since 1984 we've built enduring partnerships with customers, suppliers and our community. We set out to create the very best environment for our team so that they might deliver their unique skills to our markets.

- Public Hospitals
- Private Health
- General Practitioners
- Nurse Practitioners
- Private Hospitals (Medical, Surgical)
- Aged Care
- Accident and Emergency Clinics
- Emergency Services
- Occupational Health Services
- Community Trusts
- Physiotherapists and Sports Medicine Clinics

- Sports Clubs and Organising Bodies
- Veterinary Services
- First Aid Suppliers
- Medical Laboratories
- Specialist Clinics
- Community and Public Health Services
- Pharmacy Retail
- Industrial and Safety
- Dermatologists and Skin Clinics

OUR COMPANY AT A GLANCE:

- USL is a limited liability company, proudly New Zealand owned
- Our annual sales exceed $NZ 48 million
- Our head office and main distribution centre are based in Auckland
- The South Island is serviced from our Christchurch distribution centre
- We service 3,750 customers at all locations throughout New Zealand including all 20 of the national District Health Boards

WHAT YOU CAN EXPECT FROM US:

- We offer our customers dependability and experience they can rely on and trust.
- We deliver under IFOTIS: In-Full, On-Time, In-Specification.
- We operate a management reporting system that provides information on the frequency, recency, amount and type of purchases for all customers, and thereby enhancing their business purchasing efficiency.
- Normal guarantees apply and are rigorously honoured, and we guarantee to supply our key clients with critical stock items under IFOTIS.
- Our product range is comprehensive. It meets our customers' needs, so they can confidently have a one supplier relationship for all medical products.

In addition to the products featured in this catalogue, we also supply wound care consumables from global manyfacturers as follows:

WOUND MANAGEMENT

WOUNDCARE PRODUCTS

WOUND MANAGEMENT

THE SKIN

The skin is the largest organ in the body. It accounts for 2.5 - 3.5kg of a person's body weight and has a surface area of more than 2 square metres. Maintaining its integrity is a complex process.

THE LAYERS

The skin is divided into two primary layers; epidermis (outermost layer) and dermis (innermost layer). These two layers are separated by a structure called the basement membrane. Beneath the dermis is a layer of connective tissue called the hypodermis. Major functions of the skin are protection, immunity, thermoregulation, sensation metabolism and communication. The skin forms a protective barrier from the external environment while maintaining a haemostatic internal environment. Skin also reflects the body's general physical health.

EPIDERMIS

*   Epidermis is avascular and is made up of five layers.
*   stratum corneum (horny layer)
*   stratum licidum (clear layer)
*   stratum granulosum (granular layer)
*   stratum spinosum
*   stratum basale

DERMIS

The dermis - the thick, deeper layer of the skin is composed of collagen and elastin fibres, and an extra cellular matrix, which contributes to the skin's strength.

It is very vascular and contains nerve fibres, hair follicles, and the fibroblast cells which are critical for the formation of collagen and elastin.

It is also composed of two layers of connective tissue

*   the papillary (collagen and reticular fibres)
*   reticular dermis (network of collagen bundles)

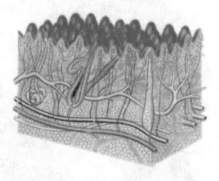

HYPODERMIS

Hypodermis forms a subcutaneous layer below the dermis. This is made up of adipose tissue which in turn provides insulation for the body. A ready energy reserve, providing additional cushioning and skin mobility over underlying structures (e.g. joints/bones).

A wound is defined by any break to the skin's surface, resulting in tissue damage.

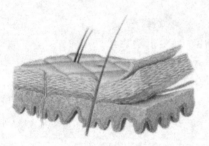

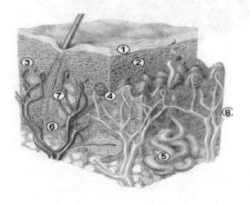

1   Horny layer
2   Prickle cell layer
3   Basal cell layer
4   Meissner's tactile corpuscles
5   Sweat gland
6   Hair follicle with hair muscle
7   Sebaceous gland
8   Free nerve ending

WOUNDS AND WOUND HEALING

TYPES OF WOUND HEALING

A wound is classified by the way it closes. A wound can close by three ways; primary, secondary or tertiary.

PRIMARY

Re-epithelialisation, in which the outer layer grows closed. Mostly superficial involving only the epidermis with no loss of tissue. Heals within 4-14 days with minimal scarring.

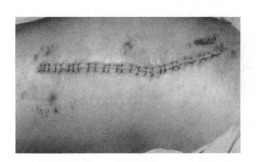

SECONDARY

Involves some degree of tissue loss with edges that can't be easily brought together. Depending on depth of damage determines whether it is a partial or full thickness wound. Wounds that heal by secondary intention fill with granulation tissue, then a scar forms and re-epithelialisation occurs. Primarily from the wound edges.

Pressure ulcers, burns, dehisced surgical wounds and traumatic injuries are all examples of this type of wound.

Typically these wounds take longer to heal, result in scarring and have more complications.

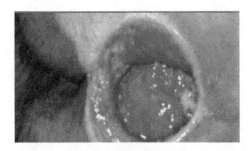

TERTIARY (DELAYED PRIMARY)

Wounds that are intentionally kept open to allow oedema or infection to resolve. These wounds are then later closed with either staples, sutures or adhesive skin closures, and can result in more scarring, due to more tissue damage.

WOUND MANAGEMENT PRINCIPLES

- define aetiology - work towards a diagnosis
- develop a management plan in conjunction with patient/family/caregiver
- assess and manage factors affecting wound and patient
- choose appropriate dressing regimen
- plan for maintenance

"To maximise healing, minimise pain and prevent cross infection through wound management that is supported by current research and best practice"

PHASES OF WOUNDS AND WOUND HEALING

The healing process begins at the instant of injury and proceeds through a repair "cascade" until healing occurs following epithelialisation. The wound healing process involves four phases which tend to overlap:

- haemostasis
- inflammation
- proliferation
- maturation

Haemostasis occurs immediately after injury and releases a multitude of growth factors into the wound to begin the healing process.

PHASES OF WOUND HEALING

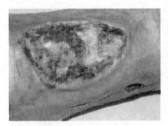  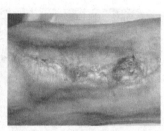

Inflammation phase (0-3 days)
- starts at the first moment of injury when capillaries contract and thrombose to facilitate haemostasis (clean-up phase)
- inflammatory response occurs following haemostasis
- influx of polymorphs protect against invasion of pathogens
- key cells are released into wound
- exudate nourishes cells and flushes out debris
- destruction and debridement by macrophages, neutrophils breakdown debris
- release of growth factors that activate fibroblasts (growth cell) and endothelial cells
- crucial phase for wound healing

Inflammation signs and symptoms
- erythema
- heat
- oedema
- discomfort
- functional disturbance

Proliferation phase (4-24 days)
- macrophages stimulate and regulate the production and work of fibroblasts
- fibroblasts produce collagen and other substances to produce new tissue
- collagen synthesis occurs to assist the formation of granulation tissue
- wound edges contract reducing wound size and epithelialisation occurs with cell migrating from wound edges and undamaged hair follicles
- angiogenesis (new capillary growth)
- granulation tissue formation (fibroblasts)
- wound contraction
- epithelialisation

Maturation phase (24 days-2 years)
- third phase of healing - main function is to increase tensile strength of wound
- collagen is converted and reorganised
- cellular activity and blood supply reduced
- decrease in vascularity and size of scar
- final stage of healing begins when the wound is covered with epithelial tissue
- maturation/ remodelling phase, lasts 6-24 months after injury
- healed tissue regains about 80% of its original strength
- Collagen fibres function is to
- reorganise
- remodel
- mature, and gain strength

  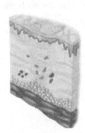

TISSUE TYPES OF WOUNDS

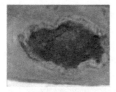
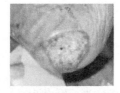

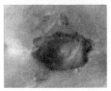

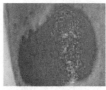
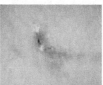

Necrotic (Black)

These wounds contain blackened areas, which are made up of dead tissue. This tissue needs to be debrided (removed) to allow healing to take place. Debridement can be achieved by surgical, mechanical, chemical means or by promoting autolysis (the breakdown of necrotic tissue by enzymes and white blood cells naturally found in tissue and wound fluid). Wound bed preparation facilitated by moist wound environment provided by some dressings, can be provided by some wound management products.

Sloughy (Yellow/Grey)

Slough is formed by the accumulation of dead cells within the wound exudate. It is important that this sloughy tissue is treated within a moist healing environment, to prevent hardening and facilitate removal.

Desloughing a wound is critical to encourage the wound bed cells to grow and heal.

Granulating (Red)

Granulation tissue is red, moist, healthy tissue that fills the wound cavity to allow for epithelialisation. It has an uneven surface due to the development of new capillaries. It requires exudate management, a moist environment, protection and support to encourage and maximise healing.

Epithialising (Pink)

Pink, translucent tissue that wrinkles when pressed. Matt finish and minimal exudate, it requires some hydration and protection especially against shear friction, and support against any further damage.

HYPERGRANULATION

This is often very vascular and bleeds easily. It has a jelly like consistency and may be quite wet. Some success has been reported using foams, antibacterial wound contact layer dressings and hypertonic saline dressings. Biopsy is necessary if it doesn't resolve with local management to rule out carcinoma.

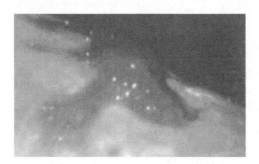

TYPES OF WOUNDS

WOUNDS CAN BE DIVIDED INTO TWO BROAD CATEGORIES, ACUTE AND CHRONIC.

ACUTE WOUNDS

Acute wounds heal in predictable phases and have excellent potential to heal, despite dressing choice. Complications are rare and there is good patient compliance. They usually heal within six weeks.

Acute wound fluid contains metabolically active cells, growth factors, appropriate levels of pro inflammatory cytokines and is biochemically balanced.

Examples of acute wounds
* traumatic wounds
* minor burns
* surgical wounds

 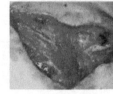

Laceration   Traumatic wound

Acute wounds are very different from chronic wounds. However a chronic wound can start off as a traumatic wound eg skin tears, then develop into chronic wound as a result of variables associated with the healing. Acute wounds are usually caused by either surgery (intentional), and/or trauma or burns. Assessment and categorisation of an acute wound should include the timeframes over which they have occurred. Is it healing in a timely, predictable, and measurable sequence? They usually heal easily without any complications.

Regardless of the cause of the acute wound, restoring anatomical structure, physiological function and the wound's normal wound appearance is the focus for acute wounds.

SURGICAL WOUNDS

An acute surgical wound is a healthy and uncomplicated break in the skin resulting from surgery.

Surgical procedures are commonly categorised by urgency, type of procedure, body system involved, degree of invasiveness, and special instrumentation.

* based on timing eg: elective surgery, emergency surgery
* based on purpose eg exploratory surgery
* by type of procedure eg amputation, reconstructive surgery, cosmetic surgery

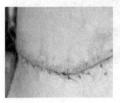 

Surgical wounds

Factors that affect the healing of a post operative wound include:
* age
* nutrition
* illness
* infection
* oxygen and circulatory status of the patient

TRAUMATIC WOUNDS

A traumatic wound is a sudden accidental injury to the skin. This can be mild or severe depending on the trauma causing incident. Examples of the types of traumatic wounds include:

* lacerations
* skin tears
* burns
* bites
* abrasions
* penetrating wounds

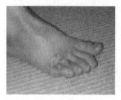 

Foot abrasion   Skin tear

"To maximise healing, minimise pain and prevent cross infection through wound management. Regardless of the cause of the acute wound restoring anatomical structure, physiological function and the wound's normal wound appearance is the focus"

CHRONIC WOUNDS

A chronic wound is a wound that does not heal in an orderly set of stages and in a predictable amount of time. Wounds that do not heal within three months are often considered chronic. In 1992, Lazarus et al defined chronic wounds as those that "fail to progress through a normal orderly and timely sequence of repair or wounds that pass through the repair process without restoring anatomic and functional results."

The most common types of chronic wounds include lower extremity leg ulcers, diabetic ulcers, and pressure ulcers. Other types of chronic wounds include skin cancers, nonhealing surgical wounds, fistulae, dermatitis or vasculitis wounds radiation wounds and burns.

Chronic wounds seem to be detained in one or more of the phases of wound healing. For example, chronic wounds often remain in the inflammatory stage for too long. Differentiated from acute wounds, there is a precise balance between production and degradation of molecules/cells such as collagen. In chronic wounds this balance is lost and degradation occurs.

Today considering wound healing as the only goal of management is short sighted. Each wound and each host are unique and have their own set of problems

Chronic wounds may never heal or may take years to do so. These wounds cause patients severe emotional and physical stress as well as creating a significant financial burden on patients and the healthcare system.

Acute and chronic wounds are at opposite ends of a spectrum of wound healing types that progress toward being healed at different rates. Critical to the management of chronic wounds is a comprehensive assessment of both patient and wound. When in doubt refer patient to specialist services for a complete wound review and managed intervention.

Classification

The vast majority of chronic wounds can be classified into three categories: venous ulcers, diabetic, and pressure ulcers. A small number of wounds that do not fall into these categories may be due to causes such as ischemia.

Venous and arterial ulcers

Venous ulcers, usually occur in the legs, account for about 70% to 90% of chronic wounds and mostly affecting the elderly. Although having stated this, there appears to be a down-trend with younger people suffering from hypertension. They are thought to be due to venous hypertension caused by improper function of valves that exist in the veins to prevent blood from flowing backward. Ischemia results from the dysfunction and, combined with reperfusion injury, causes the tissue damage that leads to the wounds.

Venous ulcer

Diabetic ulcers

Another major cause of chronic wounds, diabetes, is increasing in prevalence. Diabetics have a 15% higher risk for amputation than the general population due to chronic ulcers. Diabetes causes neuropathy, which inhibits nociception and the perception of pain. Thus patients may not initially notice small wounds to legs and feet, and may therefore fail to prevent infection or repeated injury. Further, diabetes causes immune compromise and damage to small blood vessels, preventing adequate oxygenation of tissue, which can cause chronic wounds. Pressure also plays a role in the formation of diabetic ulcers.

Diabetic ulcer

Pressure ulcers

Another leading type of chronic wound is pressure ulcers, which usually occur in people with conditions such as paralysis that inhibit movement of body parts that are commonly subjected to pressure such as the heels, shoulder blades, and sacrum. Pressure ulcers are caused by ischemia that occurs when pressure on the tissue is greater than the pressure in capillaries, and thus restricts blood flow into the area. Muscle tissue, which needs more oxygen and nutrients than skin does, can show the worst effects from prolonged pressure. As in other chronic ulcers, reperfusion injury damages tissue.

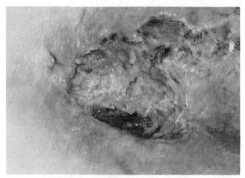

Pressure ulcer

CHRONIC WOUNDS

Signs and symptoms of chronic wounds

Chronic wound patients often report pain as dominant in their lives. It is recommended that healthcare providers handle the pain related to chronic wounds as one of the main priorities in chronic wound management (together with addressing the cause). Six out of ten venous leg ulcer patients experience pain with their ulcer, and similar trends are observed for other chronic wounds.

Persistent pain (at night, at rest, and with activity) is the main problem for patients with chronic ulcers. Frustrations regarding ineffective analgesics and plans of care that they were unable to adhere to were also identified.

Cause

In addition to poor circulation, neuropathy, and difficulty moving, factors that contribute to chronic wounds include systemic illnesses, age, poor nutrition, and repeated trauma. Comorbid ailments that may contribute to the formation of chronic wounds include vasculitis (an inflammation of blood vessels), immune suppression, pyoderma gangrenosum, and diseases that cause ischemia. Immune suppression can be caused by illnesses or medical drugs used over a long period, for example steroids. Emotional stress can also negatively affect the healing of a wound, possibly by raising blood pressure and levels of cortisol, which lowers immunity.

What appears to be a chronic wound may also be a malignancy; for example, cancerous tissue can grow until blood cannot reach the cells and the tissue becomes an ulcer. Cancer, especially squamous cell carcinoma, may also form as the result of chronic wounds, probably due to repetitive tissue damage that stimulates rapid cell proliferation.

Another factor that may contribute to chronic wounds is old age. The skin of older people is more easily damaged, and older cells do not proliferate as fast.

Repeated physical trauma plays a role in chronic wound formation by continually initiating the inflammatory cascade.

Pathophysiology

Chronic wounds may affect only the epidermis and dermis, or they may affect tissues all the way to the fascia. They may be formed originally by the same situation that cause acute wounds, such as surgery or accidental trauma, or they may form as the result of systemic infection, vascular, immune, or nerve insufficiency. The reason a wound becomes chronic is that the body's ability to deal with the damage is overwhelmed by factors such as repeated trauma, continued pressure, ischemia, or illness. Current research now understand some of the major factors that lead to chronic wounds, among which are ischemia, reperfusion injury, and bacterial colonisation.

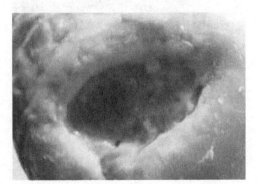

Deep pressure ulcer

Ischemia

Ischemia is an important factor in the formation and persistence of wounds, especially when it occurs repetitively (as it usually does) or when combined with a patient's old age. Ischemia causes tissue to become inflamed and cells to release factors that cause a repeated inflammatory process.

Bacterial colonisation

The host's immune response to the presence of bacteria prolongs inflammation, delays healing, and damages tissue. Infection can lead not only to chronic wounds but also to gangrene, loss of the infected limb, and death of the patient.

Treatment

Though treatment of the different chronic wound types varies slightly, appropriate treatment seeks to address the problems at the root of chronic wounds, including ischemia, bacterial load, and imbalance of proteases. Various methods exist to ameliorate these problems, including antibiotic and antibacterial use, debridement, irrigation, vacuum-assisted closure, warming, oxygenation, moist wound healing, removing mechanical stress, and adding cells or other materials to secrete or enhance levels of healing factors.

Preventing and treating infection

To lower the bacterial count in wounds, therapists may use topical antimicrobials, which kill bacteria and can also help by keeping the wound environment moist, which is important for speeding the healing of chronic wounds. A greater amount of exudate and necrotic tissue in a wound increases likelihood of infection by serving as a medium for bacterial growth away from the host's defenses.

Treating trauma and painful wounds

Persistent chronic pain associated with non-healing wounds is caused by tissue (nociceptive) or nerve (neuropathic) damage and is influenced by dressing changes and chronic inflammation. Chronic wounds take a long time to heal and patients can suffer from chronic wounds for many years. Chronic wound healing may be compromised by coexisting underlying conditions, such as venous valve backflow, peripheral vascular disease, uncontrolled oedema and diabetes mellitus.

If wound pain is not assessed and documented it may be ignored and/or not addressed properly. It is important to remember that increased wound pain may be an indicator of wound complications that need treatment, and therefore practitioners must constantly reassess the wound as well as the associated pain.

Optimal management of wounds requires holistic assessment. Documentation of the patient's pain experience is critical and may range from the use of a patient diary, (which should be patient driven), to recording pain entirely by the healthcare professional or caregiver. Effective communication between the patient and the healthcare team is fundamental to this holistic approach. The more frequently healthcare professionals' measure pain, the greater the likelihood of introducing or changing pain management practices.

At present there are few local options for the treatment of persistent pain, whilst managing the exudate levels present in many chronic wounds. Important properties of such local options are that they provide an optimal wound healing environment, while providing a constant local low dose release of ibuprofen during weartime.

If local treatment does not provide adequate pain reduction, it may be necessary for patients to seek different interventions.

"It is sad but true that there are only four facts about leg ulcers that can be stated without contradiction: they are common, their treatment is time consuming and tedious, they are not life threatening, and most surgeons would prefer someone else to be looking after them."

(Negus 1991)

Lymphoedema

Lymphoedema is swelling that results from impaired normal flow of lymph into the venous circulatory system because of a blockage. Lymphatic ulcers occur mostly on the arms and legs. These patients are vulnerable and prone to infection due to skin folds and moisture.

The goal of managing lymphatic ulcers is to:

- reduce oedema
- prevent infection

Wound management

Wound care for lymphatic ulcers is very similar to vascular ulcers. Infection is a much greater risk for the patients with Lymphoedema. Choose a dressing that can if necessary handle large amounts of fluid. Protection of the surrounding skin is critical in maintaining skin integrity.

- treat infection
- appropriate dressing selection
- multidisciplinary team approach

Lymphoedema is a chronic condition with no known cure at this stage. So positive clinical outcomes are dependent on early diagnosis and an appropriate treatment plan.

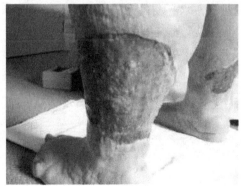

Lymphoedema

INFECTED WOUNDS

DIAGNOSIS AND MANAGEMENT

Wound infection is a serious problem. All wounds are considered contaminated as bacteria exist as part of the body's natural flora. However, this does not necessarily mean infection or sepsis will develop.

Acute and chronic wounds are both at risk of infection.

Risk factors
Risk factors can be local or systemic, these include:

Local
- foreign material
- trauma
- hypoxia
- swelling
- location of wound e.g. peri-anal
- size of wound

Systemic
- underlying disease
- smoking
- poor nutrition
- immunosupression
- alcoholism
- poor standard of hygiene
- poor general health
- multiple wounds

Bioburden
The presence of bacteria in the wound creates a burden on the wound and its ability to heal. This burden is due to the fact that bacteria compete for the limited supply of oxygen and nutrients in the wound. Achieving sterility in a wound is not possible, so the objective needs to achieve a host manageable bioburden.

Clinical signs of wound infection
- pain
- heat
- swelling
- redness
- exudate (type, consistency and/or increase in amount)

Clinical signs of systemic infection
- abnormal blood tests
- increased tiredness
- elevated temperature

CLASSIFICATION OF INFECTED WOUNDS

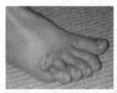 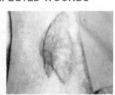  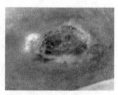

Contamination
Contamination is the presence of non-replicating micro-organisms on the wound surface. Contaminating micro-organisms are derived from normal flora (skin) external environment (linen) and contaminants (urine/faeces). There is no host reaction.

Colonisation
Refers to the presence of replicating bacteria without a host reaction or clinical signs and symptoms of infection. Bacteria in this phase do not necessitate treatment with antibiotics. Inappropriate use of antibiotics in this phase is one of the many factors contributing to the prevalence of antiobiotic-resistant organisms.

Critical colonisation
As the wound bioburden increases and further overwhelms the host, the wound reaches a period of critical colonisation. This means the wounds healing has been impeded, as a result of the bioburden.

Infection
Infection is present when the micro-organisms invade the tissues and there is a systemic response to them. The clinical appearance of the wound at this time depends on whether the wound is acute or chronic and the corresponding inflammatory responses.

MOIST WOUND HEALING

George Winter, PhD, University of London questioned if allowing wound to dry out was the best method of healing.

In 1962, George Winter published his landmark study in which he demonstrated that wounds healed faster with occlusive dressings than by air drying. A warm moist environment is necessary to encourage regranulation of epithelial tissue and local production of vascular endothelial growth factor (VEGF). Occlusive dressings are designed to create a moist micro-environment that promotes wound healing.

Results: Wounds that had been covered by polymer film, epithelialised twice as quickly as the wounds exposed to air.

Winter postulated that epithelial cells in dry wounds have to negotiate the scab, consuming energy and time, whereas in moist wounds they migrate freely across a moist, vascular wound surface. Winter's theory has been supported by other studies in addition other studies provided evidence that a moist environment can accelerate the inflammatory response, leading to faster cell proliferation and wound healing in deeper dermal wounds.

The principle of moist wound healing mimics the function of the epidermis. Our body is mainly composed of water, and the natural environment of a cell is moist; therefore, a dry cell is a dead cell. The diagram below demonstrates the benefits of moist wound healing from use of an occlusive dressing.

The benefits of a moist environment for wound healing are:

- increases the rate of healing and improves the cosmetic result
- better manages exudate
- decreases pain - moist wound bed insulates and protects nerve endings thereby reducing pain
- enhanced autolytic debridement - debrides the wound effectively
- prevents scab formation - scabs form a physical barrier to healing - decreased dehydration and cell death (neutrophils, macrophages, and fibroblast necessary for wound healing cannot thrive in a dry environment)
- increased angiogenesis
- increased re-epithelialisation (dry crusted wounds decrease supply of blood and nutrients which thus results in a barrier to cell migration and slowing of epithelialisation.)
- reduces scarring

Moist wound healing is considered to be the ideal environment for optimal wound healing. The work of zoologist George Winter (1927–1981) stimulated a great deal of research into the development of new types of dressings that completely revolutionised the care of wounds. Research before and since Winter's work suggests that moisture under occlusive dressings promotes healing through moisture itself, some of the components of wound exudate, and the presence of low oxygen tension. Occlusive dressings increase cell proliferation and activity by retaining vital proteins and cytokines contained within wound exudate produced in response to injury. Although there have been some concerns regarding increased infection in a moist wound environment, these concerns appear to be unfounded.

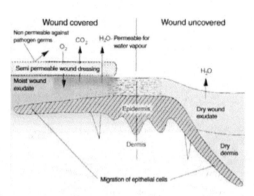

Diagram of a protected and an unprotected skin wound

Cell stripping and trauma caused during dry dressing change

Wound dressings

- the ideal dressing is one that:
- maintains a moist environment/moisture balance
- allows gaseous exchange
- provides thermal insulation
- provides a barrier to pathogens
- does not promote infection
- does not shed fibres or leak toxic substances
- protects against mechanical trauma eg; shearing and friction
- allows removal without traumatising new tissue
- is easy to apply, comfortable to wear and adaptable to body parts
- does not interfere with body function
- is cost effective

PATIENT
ASSESSMENT
AND WOUND
DOCUMENTATION

PATIENT AND WOUND ASSESSMENT

ACCURATE ASSESSMENT OF THE PATIENT AND THE WOUND

Assessment provides the foundation for the wound management plan for the patient.

Accurate assessment and regular reassessment of all aspects of the wound and patient should be undertaken on admission and at each dressing change in order to monitor effectiveness of treatment regime and optimise wound healing. This can also be effectively achieved by the use of periodic photographs giving a visual record to support written documentation.

Reduce or eliminate causative factors
*   pressure, shearing forces, friction, circulatory impairment, etc
*   identify and manage infection

Provide systematic support for wound healing
*   good nutrition - dietary supplements may be required
*   control of systemic conditions. e.g. blood sugar levels, oedema, cardiac disease, circulatory disorders

ASSESSMENT OF THE PATIENT

An important aspect of wound management is to assess the patient as a whole and should include:-
*   general physical condition and age
*   activity level
*   urinary and faecal continence
*   other diseases e.g. diabetes, cardiac function
*   current medications, treatments
*   self care ability
*   level of pain/tolerance
*   location of wound/ability to reach dressing site
*   skin condition

DESCRIBING AND DOCUMENTING A WOUND
*   mobility level
*   nutritional status
*   sensory functioning
*   compliance with treatment

The initial cause of the wound and duration of treatment when describing a wound in the patient's clinical record/wound assessment chart should include:
*   type of wound and location
*   aim of treatment; to promote healing/palliative
*   wound size
*   presence of necrotic tissue and/or slough
*   condition of wound bed, surrounding skin and wound edges
*   amount of exudate/drainage (noting any odour)
*   presence of pain
*   current dressing regime
*   the progress of the wound healing according to the resident and/or carer, (this can further be evidenced with the use of photographs)
*   ability to educate patients/family/caregiver

WOUND ASSESSMENT TOOLS

(T.I.M.E. FRAMEWORK)

TIME is an acronym to identify and manage the wounds imbalances therein improving patient outcomes.

TIME includes:

*   **Tissue management**
*   **Inflammation and infection control**
*   **Moisture balance and wound**
*   **Edge assessment**

This simple tool is a great reference to clearly establish and prioritise the care and treatment regimes required for each individual patient and wound.

(H.E.I.D.I. FRAMEWORK)

HEIDI is a holistic assessment tool which encompasses the patient and the wound, and all those factors influencing healing.

HEIDI includes:

*   **History**
*   **Examination**
*   **Investigate**
*   **Diagnose**
*   **Indicators for healing**

Prior to assessing the wound thorough assessment of the patient to understand all the systemic and local factors that will affect healing is essential.

CHARACTERISTICS OF EXUDATE

Amount
Exudate is difficult to measure accurately, often described as light, moderate or heavy. Heavy exudate may result in electrolyte imbalance. It may be useful to use a wound drainage bag if possible.

Dry: Wound bed is dry. There is no visible moisture. This may be the environment of choice for ischaemic wounds

Moist: Small amounts of fluid are visible when the dressing is removed. Dressing changes are appropriate for dressing type

Wet: Small amounts of fluid are visible when dressing is removed; the primary dressing is extensively marked

Saturated: Primary dressing is wet and strike through is occurring; dressing change is required more frequently or the dressing type needs to change

Leaking: Dressings are saturated and exudate is escaping from primary/secondary dressings; dressing change is required more frequently or the dressing type needs to change.

WOUND DOCUMENTATION CHART

When performing a thorough wound and skin assessment, a pictorial record is helpful to help identify the wound site or sites. Using the patient and wound document chart example shown here helps to document and record the patient's wound and healing progress.

Patient and Wound Document Chart

HARTMANN

Surname: _____   First Name: _____   Date: _____

General Assessment

Influencing Factors:
Age: _____
Underlying Disease: _____
_____
_____
_____

Malignancy: _____
Diabetes: _____
Vascular/Arterial Function: _____
_____

Smoking: _____
Psychological State: _____

Obesity/Cachexia: _____
Radiation Therapy: _____
Other: _____

Medication:
Steroids: _____
_____
Cytotoxics: _____
_____
Immunosuppressants: _____
_____
Antibiotics: _____
_____
NSAIDS: _____
_____
Other: _____
_____

Nutritional Status:
Good: _____
Average: _____
Poor: _____
Other: _____

Mobility:
Mobile: _____
Slight Impairment: _____
Gross Impairment: _____
Immobile: _____

Diagnostic Investigations:
_____
_____
_____
_____

Wound Assessment

Wound Type:
Acute: _____
Chronic: _____

Aetiology: _____
_____
_____
_____

Duration Of Wound: _____
_____

Location: _____
_____

Dimensions: _____
Width-cm: _____
Length-cm: _____
Depth-cm: _____

Clinical Appearance: _____
Necrotic: _____
Sloughy: _____
Granulating: _____
Epitheliating: _____
Hypergranulating: _____

Exudate Amount: _____
Dry: _____
Moist: _____
Wet: _____
Saturated: _____
Leaking: _____

Exudate Type:
Serous: _____
Haemoserous: _____
Blood: _____
Purulent: _____

Condition Of Wound: _____
Clean: _____
Contaminated: _____
Infected: _____

Odour: _____
Nil: _____
Present: _____

Surrounding Skin:
Healthy: _____
Erythema: _____
Oedematous: _____
Macerated: _____
Fragile: _____
Dry: _____
Dermatitis/Eczema: _____
Other: _____

Pain: (Pain Scale 1/10)
Severity: _____
Frequency: _____

Treatment Plan

Hydrate: _____ ☐
Decrease bioburden: _____ ☐
Absorption: _____ ☐
Debridement: _____ ☐
Protection: _____ ☐
Other: _____ ☐

Wound Cleansing:
Sterile Normal Saline: _____
Shower: _____
Tap Water: _____

Dressing Products:
Primary Dressing: _____

Secondary Dressing: _____

Dressing Retention Aid: _____

Notes: _____
_____
_____
_____
_____
_____
_____
_____
_____
_____
_____
_____
_____

PAIN AND WOUND MANAGEMENT

PAIN - THE FIFTH VITAL SIGN

THE FIVE VITAL SIGNS

- blood pressure
- pulse
- respiration
- temperature
- pain

WHAT IS PAIN?

Pain is an unpleasant sensory and emotional experience associated with actual or potential tissue damage or described in terms of such damage. *International Association for the Study of Pain [IASP]* The fact remains that pain is an alarm signal telling us that something in the body is wrong.

TWO MAJOR TYPES OF PAIN

Nociceptive (tissue) pain

- results from tissue damage (mechanical, thermal or chemical trauma to peripheral nerve fibres)
- is mediated at nociceptors widely distributed in skin tissue, bone, muscle and connective tissue

Nociceptive pain is described as sharp, dull, aching or throbbing pain.

Neuropathic (nerve) pain

- damage or dysfunction to the peripheral or central nervous system
- faulty signals are sent to the brain and experienced as pain

Neuropathic pain is described as a burning, tingling, shooting, electric-like, or lightning-like pain.

SENSORY RECEPTORS IN THE SKIN

- pain
- touch/pressure
- temperature
- vibration

Every cm² of skin contains around

- 200 pain receptors (nociceptors)
- 15 receptors for pressure
- 6 for cold
- 1 for warmth

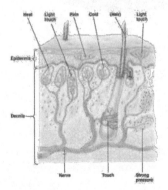

WHAT CAUSES PAIN?

- injury to cells result in chemical release which in turn leads to inflammation
- trauma/injury initiates immediate nerve impulses to brain

Clinical symptoms associated with nociceptor (inflammatory) response to tissue injury

- increased temperature
- pain
- bruising
- swelling

All beyond the immediate zone of injury.

This wound shows classic signs of inflammation with the reaction depicted beyond the injury site.

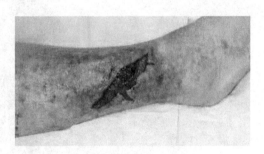

"Pain is a personal and subjective experience that can only be felt by the sufferer."
Katz and Melzack

"Pain is whatever the experiencing person says it is and exists whenever they say it does." *McCaffery*

EWMA KEY FINDINGS

- dressing removal is considered to be the time of most pain
- dried out dressings and adherent products are most likely to cause pain and trauma at dressing changes
- products designed to be non-traumatic are most frequently used to prevent tissue trauma
- gauze is most likely to cause pain, new products such as hydrogels, hydrofibres, alginates and soft silicone dressings are least likely to cause pain
- awareness of product range and ability to select dressings is highly variable between countries
- use of valid pain assessment tool is considered a low priority in assessment, with greater reliance on body language and non-verbal cues

MAIN CONSIDERATIONS AT DRESSING CHANGE

- Prevent wound trauma
- Prevent pain
- Prevent infection
- Prevent skin damage
- Other

FACTORS CONTRIBUTING TO PAIN

- Dried out dressings
- Products that adhere
- Adhesive dressings
- Cleansing
- Previous experience
- Fear of hurting
- Packed gauze

WOUNDS ARE PAINFUL (AND NOT JUST DURING DRESSING CHANGES!)

- 64-82% of leg ulcers
- 48% of diabetic foot ulcers
- 59% of pressure ulcers

PAIN ALTERS PHYSIOLOGY OF THE BODY BY CREATING STRESS REACTION

- stress of pain creates a catabolic reaction (breaking down of fat, protein and carbohydrates for immediate energy use)
- this catabolic response inhibits healing - instead of building tissue, the body is breaking it down

UNRELIEVED PAIN WEAKENS PATIENT

- "breakdown" processes takes lots of energy
- sleep deprivation is a common side effect of pain and interferes with healing
- unrelieved pain causes a suppression of the immune function because the body wears out responding to the pain
- increases susceptibility to infection

Relationship between poor wound healing and pain is well documented.

WOUND PAIN

- procedure related pain
- dressing change (removal from peri-woundand wound bed)
- wound bed cleansing
- peri-wound cleansing
- mechanical debridement
- chronic, always present, wound pain

REFERENCE
Understanding wound pain and trauma: an international perspective

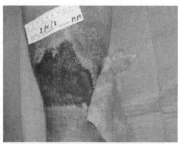
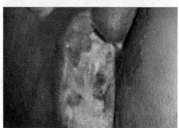

PAIN - THE FIFTH VITAL SIGN

PHYSIOLOGICAL PAIN PATHWAY

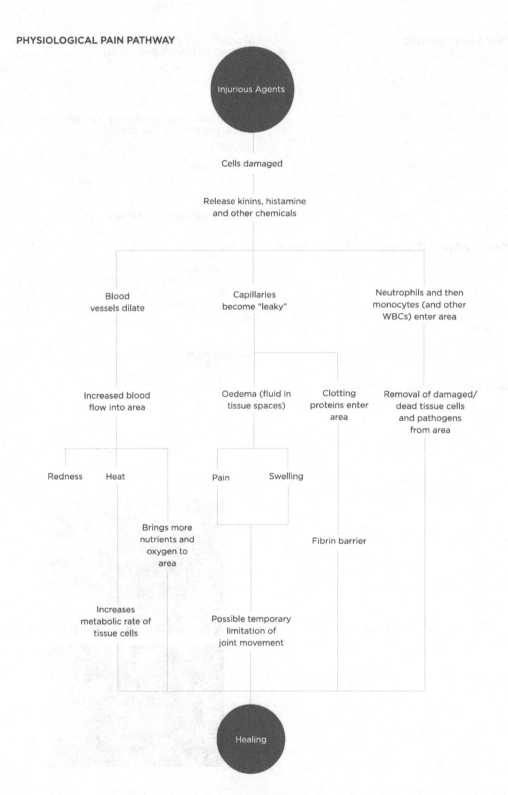

NUTRITION AND WOUND HEALING

NUTRITION AND WOUND HEALING

Nutrition is a fundamental part of normal cell function, integrity and tissue repair. Lack of adequate nutrition has been associated with increased morbidity and mortality in medical and surgical patients.

Nursing has the primary responsibility for the initial nutritional assessment across all settings - hospital primary care and aged care facilities. Early nutritional assessment is critical in an effort to identify those individuals at-risk for and experiencing malnutrition. It's vital in providing positive wound healing outcomes.

DEFINITION

Malnutrition is undernutrition or overnutrition that is caused by a deficit or excess of nutrients in the diet.

NUTRIENT NEEDS FOR HEALING

Normal healing requires adequate protein, fat, and carbohydrates, as well as vitamins and minerals. Deficiencies in any of these nutrients may result in delayed or impaired healing.

With wound injuries, more calories are needed than in an uninjured state. Calories are needed purely for energy alone and normal bodily functions. When an injury is part of the patient, then their nutritional needs should be assessed and revised accordingly.

Nutritional assessment provides the basis for developing a nutritional plan. A physical examination and patient history are essential in obtaining the overall nutritional status of each patient.

Nutritional support should provide a balanced intake of necessary nutrients based on the person's energy and protein requirements.

The patient at risk or with existing malnutrition needs to be brought to the attention of the health care team so appropriate support can be provided. This includes referral to a dietician and/or physician.

NUTRITION AND WOUND HEALING

Malnutrition causes delays in wound healing and substantially can impact on the wound's ability to heal. When a patient is debilitated by their wound their need for extra nutrition increases proportionally.

Some critical factors to consider when assessing a patient's nutritional status are:

Amino acids – derived from protein found in meat, fish, poultry, diary products and lentils. Arginine (see table below) exisits as an amino acid and supports collagen formation.

Lipids – are fats and an excellent source of energy and can either be saturated or non-saturated. Saturated fats are responsible for raising blood cholesterol and mono or poly-unsaturated fats help lower blood cholesterol. Essential fatty acids can be obtained from whole grains, mono or poly-unsaturated oils, nuts and fish.

Carbohydrates – are essential for the functioning of cellular energy. Critical for fibroblasts, collagen, leucocytes, synthesis of DNA and RNA and nutrient absorption.

Vitamin C – is also known as absorbic acid. Important in fibroblast production and immune responses thereby help enhance wound healing. Can gain this vitamin from kiwifruit, citrus fruits, capsicum, strawberries and rockmelon.

Also iron and vitamins A, B, D (sunlight derived), K, and E play an important role in nutrition and wound healing, as well as trace elements.

SUMMARY

Nutritional assessment and support play an important role in successful wound healing. All patients with wounds should have their nutritional status evaluated and a plan put in place, which should be re-assessed regularly for effectiveness.

NUTRIENTS ESSENTIAL TO WOUND HEALING

Arginine
* helps new skin tissue production
* helps increase blood flow to wound bed
* enhances immune system activity

Protein
* provides high levels of protein to help wound healing. wounds require 25-50% more protein intake
* helps build and maintain lean muscle mass

Vitamins A, C and antioxidants
* enhance wound healing by reducing cellular damage caused by chemical reactions
* play an important role on collagen synthesis

Zinc
* required for wound repair
* required for tissue growth, skin integrity, cell mediated immunity and generalised host defence

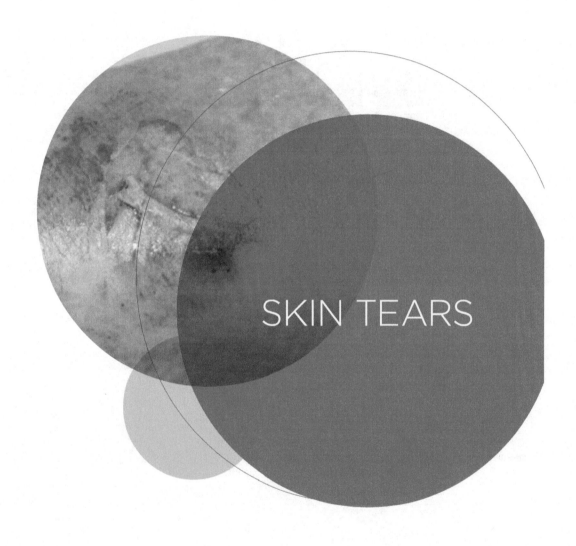

SKIN TEARS

SKIN TEARS

DISTRIBUTION OF SKIN TEARS

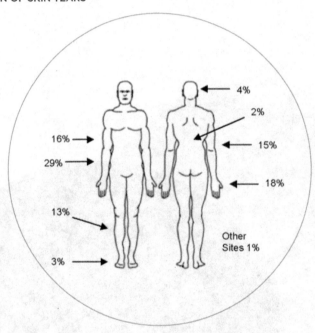

4%
2%
16%
29%
15%
18%
13%
Other
Sites 1%
3%

RATIONALE

Skin tears are usually quite painful, and are the most common wound type amongst the elderly. It is estimated that at least 1.5 million skin tears occur annually among institutionalised adults in the USA, with 14% of patients suffering from skin tears each month. A combined analysis suggests that the average distribution of skin tears is: head 4%, biceps area 16%, elbow 15%, forearm 29%, top of hand 18%, trunk/back 2%, shin 13%, top of foot 3%, and other sites 1%. They can become infected and may heal slowly in compromised patients. As our population ages, it is becoming increasingly important for all health care providers to learn how to manage skin tears to promote quick, pain-free healing while preventing infection and other complications.

DEFINITION

In 1993, Payne and Martin published their revised definition of a skin tear:

"A traumatic wound occurring principally on the extremities of older adults, as a result of friction alone or shearing and friction forces which separate the epidermis from the dermis (partial thickness wound) or which separate both the epidermis and dermis from the underlying structures (full thickness wound)."

Payne and Martin also developed the standard system for categorising skin tears (detailed on page 30).

PATHOPHYSIOLOGY OF SKIN TEARS

Skin tears become increasingly common with age because:

- the skin thins internally and contains less subcutaneous fat, especially at the shins, face and back of the hands

- elasticity is reduced because collagen and elastin in the skin degenerates

- natural lubrication is diminished due to reduced functioning of the sweat and sebaceous glands

- the capillaries become fragile and disorganised, leading to easy bruising and reduced blood supply

- the dermal-epidermal junction is weakened because the rete ridges that keep the dermis and epidermis locked together are flattened, making aging skin especially susceptible to injury from friction and shear; when the epidermis is moved, the dermis may remain stationary rather than moving with it

Steroid use thins the skin and anticoagulants damage capillaries, so younger persons on these medications are also at increased risk for skin tears.

RISK FACTORS

Individual factors which increase susceptibility to skin tears include:

- nutritional deficits, particularly insufficient protein and essential fatty acids, which are vital to skin health

- oedema or dehydration, which compromise skin health and make it more susceptible to injury

- having visible evidence of a fragile skin capillary bed, such as red splotches, purpura or bruising (skin tears are more likely to occur over such areas)

- age over 85 is associated with the most pronounced skin changes and the most risk of skin tears

- sensory and cognitive deficits, especially verbal communication deficits

- stiffness, from contractures, Parkinson's Disease, etc, because transfers are more difficult

- ambulatory impairments – 18% of all skin tears occur while transferring patients, 25% are wheelchair injuries, and patients requiring total care for all activities of daily living are at highest risk for skin tears

- about 50% of the time the cause of a skin tear is not determinable

As might be expected, the individuals most at risk for skin tears are those with a past history of skin tears

PREVENTION

Prevention of skin tears is two-pronged:

- improving skin health and decreasing the risk of trauma.

- Implementing prevention protocols can result in a significant reduction in skin tears and is financially sound.

Steps for improving skin health

- ordinary soaps and alcohol dry the skin, exacerbating the problems of the elderly. Use soaps sparingly, and chose soaps with a pH of about 5.5 which contain an emollient or humectant

- bathe patients gently, using warm rather than hot water, soaking rather than scrubbing off crusts

- pat skin, rather than rubbing it dry

- apply a once-daily formula moisturising cream to the skin immediately after the bath to lock in moisture

- correct underlying dehydration and nutritional deficiencies, paying special attention to protein, essential fatty acids, and zinc

Steps for minimising injury from trauma

- encourage older adults to wear long sleeves and long pants to provide a layer of protection for their skin

- secure padding to bed rails, wheelchair arms and leg supports, and other furniture and equipment to protect patients from injury due to bumps

- use no tape, or only tapes that are easily removed on elderly patients, preferring stockinettes and wraps for securing dressings and drains. If tape or bordered dressings are used, pull the edge parallel to the patient's skin to loosen the adhesive bond before lifting the dressing away

- teach family members and health care workers proper lifting and turning techniques to prevent friction, shearing and bruising. Older adults must be handled very gently. Use facial cues to determine if pain is present

- provide a well-lit environment with furniture arranged thoughtfully to minimise bumps and falls

TREATMENT AND PREVENTION OF SKIN TEARS

Goal: The desired outcome of this is to maximise healing while minimising complications and pain associated with skin tears. Implementation of the prevention aspects of the protocol is expected to result in significant cost savings due to a diminished incidence of skin tears. Treatment costs may also be reduced.

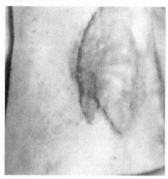

Skin tear

"A traumatic wound occurring principally on the extremities of older adults, as a result of friction alone or shearing and friction forces which separate the epidermis from the dermis (partial thickness wound) or which separate both the epidermis and dermis from the underlying structures (full thickness wound)."

SKIN TEARS

Payne-Martin classification system (revised 1993):

Category I: Skin tears without tissue loss

A. LINEAR TYPE

A linear skin tear is a full thickness wound occuring in a wrinkle or furrow of the skin. Both the epidermis and the dermis are pulled apart as if an incision has been made, exposing the tissue below

B. FLAP TYPE

A flap type skin tear is a partial thickness wound in which the epidermal flap can be completely approximated or approximated so that no more than one (1) millimetre of dermis is exposed

Category II: Skin tears with partial tissue loss

A. SCANT TISSUE LOSS TYPE

A skin tear with scant tissue loss is a partial thickness wound in which 25% or less of the epidermal flap is lost and in which at least 75% or more of the dermis is covered by the flap

 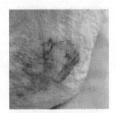

B. MODERATE-TO-LARGE TISSUE LOSS TYPE

A skin tear with moderate-to-large tissue loss is a partial thickness wound in which more than 25% of the epidermal flap is lost and in which more than 25% of the dermis is exposed

Category III: Skin tears with complete tissue loss

A skin tear with complete tissue loss is a partial thickness wound in which the epidermal flap is absent

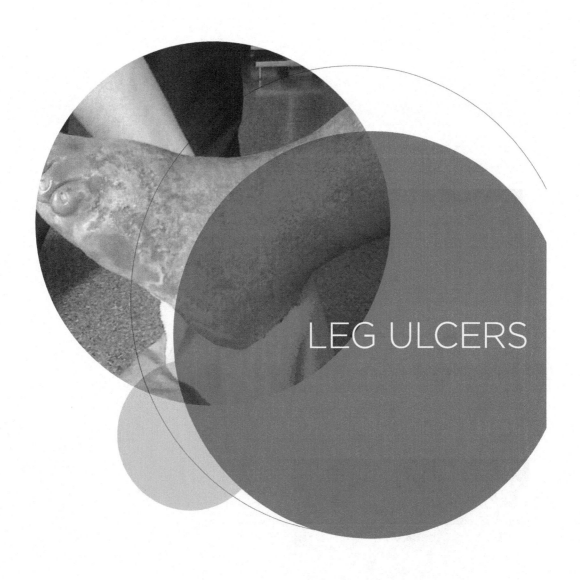

LEG ULCERS

VENOUS LEG ULCERS

OVERVIEW

Causes

It is thought that alterations in blood flow due to venous hypertension from chronic venous insufficiency (CVI) cause white blood cells to adhere to the walls of the smaller vessels of the lower leg. The white blood cells may plug the vessels or leak from them and release tissue destroying enzymes and inflammatory mediators into the tissues. Venous ulcers are likely caused by a prolonged and chaotic local inflammatory state induced by this aspect of venous hypertension. Mild trauma can also precipitate venous leg ulcers in patients with CVI. Venous hypertension causes fluid to leak into the tissues; this oedema compresses the capillaries, decreasing blood flow to the skin and increasing damage. Chronic inflammation prevents venous ulcers from healing at the pace of acute wounds.

Characteristics

Venous ulcers are predominantly in the ankle or lower calf (gaiter

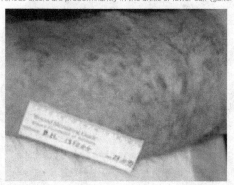

Varicose veins resulting in venous hypertension

area). The medial ankle is by far the most common site because the long saphenous vein is more superficial and has the greatest curvature there and because this is the area of the highest pressure within the entire venous system. Venous ulcers tend to produce copious exudate when uncompressed and are usually

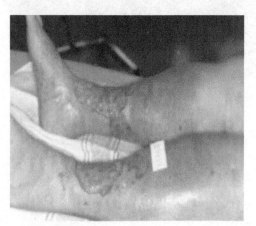

Venous leg ulcers

shallow, irregular, and often have a yellow fibrous bed.

Risk factors for venous ulcers

Patients with venous ulcers can have an increased tendency for blood to clot (thrombophilia), which is often a congenital condition. Other risk factors for ulceration include:

*   history of phlebitis or deep vein thrombosis (DVT)
*   history of leg trauma, such as a fracture, but even minor trauma can cause vessel damage
*   vigorous exercise (which may cause microtrauma)
*   CVI or varicose veins in the patient or maternal family history
*   pregnancy, obesity or ascites, all of which cause increased abdominal pressure, femoral vein compression, and decreased mobility
*   multiple pregnancies
*   greater height, which increases venous system pressure
*   recent lower leg oedema, which may be caused by chronic heart failure or medications
*   diabetes, which decreases skin health
*   increasing age, because valve damage is permanent and cumulative
*   poor calf muscle function or decreased range of motion (ROM) in the foot. Standing or sitting for prolonged periods of time with the feet dependent dramatically increases susceptibility to ulceration.

Assessing oedema

Lower leg circumferences should be measured at the widest point and at 2.5cm above the malleolus. It is important to rule out systemic and reversible causes of oedema, such as medication reactions, heart or liver failure and low protein. Suspect accompanying lymphoedema, if skin at the base of the second toe is so thick that you cannot pick up a fold of it (Stemmer Sign). Oedema caused by lymphoedema does not respond significantly to limb elevation. With standard compression, fluid from lymphoedema may simply move to proximal areas. Refer patients for testing to rule out lymphoedema if oedema does not improve despite elevation and compression.

Biopsy

Although venous disease is the most common cause of leg ulcers, it is by no means the only cause. Sickle cell, arterial insufficiency, rheumatologic disorders, cancer, infection, medication reactions, vasculitis and a host of other systemic illnesses can lead to leg ulcers which mimic venous ulcers but require different interventions. It is important to note that the chronic inflammation in venous ulcers can cause them to degenerate into a malignancy. So, if there is no significant decrease in size or increase in granulation of the wound after six weeks of treatment as described in this protocol, a biopsy of the wound base and margin should be considered to confirm the pathology of the leg ulcer.

Improve nutrition

Protein deficiency can result in leg oedema. Adequate levels of protein, vitamin A, vitamin C and zinc are needed for wound healing. Wound patients require 25–35 kcal/kg/day with 1.0–1.2 g/kg/day protein. Supplementation should be individualised.

VENOUS LEG ULCERS

Initial studies show that the slow healing of almost 50% of all chronic leg ulcers could be due to elevated levels of the amino acid. Appropriate supplementation with high amounts of vitamins B6, B12 and folic acid can dramatically aid in improving healing and preventing recurrence of leg ulcers in affected individuals.

Venous dermatitis skin treatment
Due to the risk of sensitivity, legs should be washed with warm water. Venous dermatitis may require treatment with measured amounts of zinc paste bandages.

Surgery
Grafting or venous surgery should be considered for wounds that do not heal with appropriate wound care. Recently, minimally invasive vein surgery (MIVS) techniques such as radiofrequency ablation, endovenous laser, and foam sclerotherapy are less expensive and less risky than previous surgical treatments to correct venous hypertension; some can be done in the doctor's office. Surgical correction of the venous reflux may not improve venous ulcer healing rates, but it dramatically reduces the recurrence of ulcers and should be considered in ulcer patients with superficial venous insufficiency using compression bandaging. The best surgical candidates are patients with sufficient mobility to activate the calf muscle pump, and predominantly superficial or perforator venous incompetence (this includes 50% of venous ulcer patients). Duplex scanning locates the venous system abnormalities.

Patients are advised to continue wearing compression following surgery. Although skin grafting can temporarily close clean wounds, grafted wounds tend to recur unless the underlying venous disease is treated surgically, even if the patient uses compression hosiery.

Venous wound infections
Surface wound contamination is common to all venous wounds. Wound infection has recently been redefined as multiplication of invasive microorganisms in viable wound tissue resulting in abnormal effects or tissue injury. Chronic wound infections are now divided into two categories: superficial and deep. Systemic antibiotic treatment is usually reserved for deep infections. Superficial venous wound infection (increased bacterial burden) signs and symptoms include:

* delayed healing despite appropriate compression therapy
* abnormal, friable or absent granulation tissue
* change in quantity, viscosity or odour of drainage

* increase or change in ulcer pain

Deep wound infections may also cause:

* pain, warmth, redness and swelling of the surrounding skin
* newly formed ulcers or wound bed extension within inflamed margins of pre-existing ulcers
* ulcer enlargement

Assessing infection in venous ulcers is extremely difficult. Sensitivity reactions may look like infection. Venous leg ulcers may have inflammation, induration, swelling, pain, warmth, foul odour, copious drainage and tenderness to touch without being infected. A change in sensation around the wound may be the only sign of infection in immunocompromised patients.

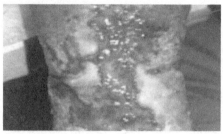

Venous ezcema

VENOUS INSUFFICIENCY PATHWAY

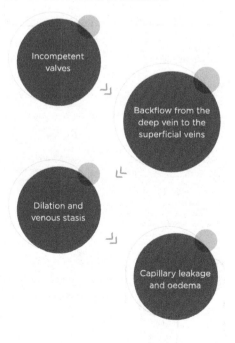

Incompetent valves

Backflow from the deep vein to the superficial veins

Dilation and venous stasis

Capillary leakage and oedema

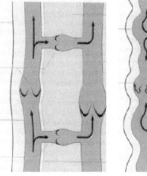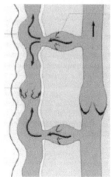

Normal venous return   Abnormal venous return

LEG ULCER MANAGEMENT

MANAGEMENT

Management of venous hypertension helps prevent venous ulcer formation and is the foundation of venous wound treatment.

Elevation
Continuous bed rest with leg elevation will decrease oedema from CVI, but this is rarely practical.

Exercise
Standing or sitting for prolonged periods of time with the feet dependent should be avoided, as should vigorous exercise, but a daily walking program (30 minutes of brisk walking twice a day) should be encouraged to improve circulation and for quality of life. Gait training and simple restorative exercises to increase the ankle joint range of motion and strength (see diagrams) address the underlying causes of CVI. Increases in the depth of breathing during exercise aid in venous and lymphatic return. Even nonambulatory patients can increase blood flow and decrease oedema through passive foot/ankle/lower limb exercises and weight bearing with assistance. Rocking in a chair, calf pump action while lying supine, and deep breathing all help with venous return. In contrast, prolonged standing or sitting, wearing high heels and crossing of the legs reduces venous return.

Compression
The cornerstone of chronic venous insufficiency therapy is

Every hour do 30 foot raises   Every hour do 30 foot extensions

graduated lower leg compression. Graduated compression increases the blood flow velocity and lymph drainage, so it works on the most probable cause of the venous ulceration (leakage of injurious substances from the vessels) as well as decreasing superficial venous system pressure and reducing oedema. The reduction in venous hypertension and oedema that compression affords results in decreased leakage of exudate and increased cutaneous blood flow. Valves that are not touching because of venous distension are pushed back into approximation by compression. Patients who wear graduated compression consistently have significantly improved healing rates and decreased recurrence rates. Many also report relief of venous pain. Compression for life is essential to prevent recurrence. Two basic types of compression systems are used

for treating chronic venous insufficiency: elastic and inelastic.

Specific methods of applying graduated compression are discussed further in this section.

Medication and co-morbidity management
Patients may need alternatives to medications that cause oedema.

Weight loss
A weight reduction program is advisable for obese patients, and bariatric surgery may be indicated for super-obese (BMI>60) venous ulcer patients.

Avoid vasoconstriction
Vasoconstriction decreases peripheral blood flow. Causes of vasoconstriction, such as cold environment, dehydration, stress, pain, and cigarette smoking should be eliminated.

Pain control
Pain in venous ulcers is usually caused by tissue damage and the resultant inflammation. Inflammation leads to more pain, even with usually non-painful stimuli, by exciting the nociceptors. Pain causes decreased mobility, which causes increased ulceration, which causes more pain. Pain causes a stress reaction, which increases the risk of ulcer infection and creates another destructive cycle because infection is a major cause of pain.

Assess location, intensity, quality, and duration of pain, as well as pain precipitators and pain relievers. Manage pain with leg elevation and compression, PolyMem® dressings, analgesics, relaxation, etc.

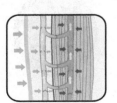

External compression vein support

ARTERIAL ULCERS

OVERVIEW

Arterial ulcers are also known as ischemic ulcers. They occur as a result of severe tissue ischemia due to arterial insufficiency. They are known to be extremely painful and have potential to represent potential limb loss. They account for approximately 5-20% of all leg ulcers. The management of these ulcers is multifaceted and unless tissue perfusion is restored or improved progress onto extensive infection and/or gangrene is likely.

Arterial insufficiency occurs when arterial blood flow is restricted or obstructed. Blockage can occur in any artery and appear anywhere along the arterial branches from the aorta to the capillary.

Causes

The most common cause of arterial ulcers is atherosclerosis involving the peripheral circulation. The most commonly affected vessels are the aortic, femoral, iliac, and popliteal arteries. Patients at high risk for developing atherosclerosis include men, cigarette smokers, and those individuals with hypertension, diabetes mellitus or hyperlipidemia. Advanced age places the patient at even more risk.

Atherosclerotic disease causes plaque formation and a hardening of the vessel wall. An occluded artery results in a chronic reduction in blood flow which impacts on the limb tissues.

Indicators of critical limb ischaemia

*   nonpalpable pulse
*   ankle brachial index <4
*   rest pain
*   ulceration or gangrene

Assessment

Assessment of a patient with an arterial ulcer needs to be very thorough. A complete patient history needs to be taken along with a physical examination. History of the pain caused by arterial insufficiency is important to document. Gather relevant information about the type of pain experienced - is the pain at rest or when the foot is elevated or hanging.

Diagnostic testing for arterial ulcers should be completed to assess arterial flow to extremities before deciding on best management plan. Some commonly used testing methods are:

*   duplex ultrasonography
*   ankle-brachial index
*   arteriography

Management of arterial ulcers

The goal of management is to improve perfusion to the ulcer supplying essential oxygenation and nutrients to support the healing process.

The prognosis for the wound to heal is directly related to the ability to provide reperfusion of the tissues.

The specific interventions for the patient are determined by the severity of the ischaemia and the patient's overall health. Some of the interventions include:

*   surgical options eg arterial bypass grafts
*   medication to reduce thrombotic events eg anticoagulants
*   angioplasty and stents
*   amputation (usually last resort)

Arterial ulcers

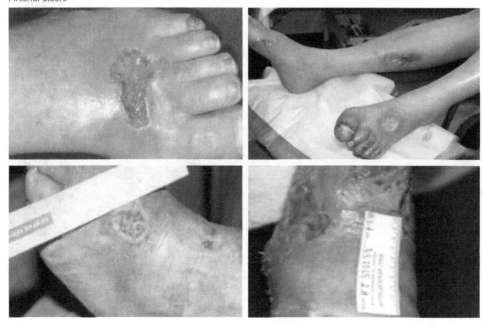

DIABETIC ULCERS

DIABETIC ULCERS

Diabetes Mellitus is a metabolic disorder that results in hyperglycaemia as a result of increased insulin. Due to this impaired perfusion and other complications eg infection, neuropathy, repeated trauma, healing of the diabetic ulcer is extremely challenging. The lower extremity metabolic changes that occur as a result of diabetes exacerbate neuropathy (nerve pain).

Insulin is critical for transporting glucose into the cells where it is used as fuel or stored as glycogen. An insulin deficiency compromises important functions and therefore diabetics are much more susceptible to developing foot ulcers.

Peripheral neuropathy is the primary cause of diabetic foot ulcers. Neuropathy is a nerve disorder that results in impaired or lost function in the tissues served by the affected nerve. This results in loss of sensation, loss of motor function and loss of autonomic functions. Typically this starts affecting the feet and hands first then progresses towards the knees and elbows respectively.

As sensation declines the patient risks injury. Their normal reactions to pain and stimuli do not function as before so injury occurs particularly of the feet.

Mechanical forces
Pressure friction and shear are the mechanical forces that can contribute to diabetic ulcers.

Bony prominences are most commonly affected including the metatarsal heads, great toe and the heel. Or the shearing effect of a loose shoe against the skin and underlying structures.

Peripheral vascular disease
Is a major problem in patients with diabetes because the accompanying lack of oxygen and perfusion of tissues significantly impairs healing.

Risk factors
Identifying risk factors is an important part of prevention. Loss of sensation is the biggest factor but other risk factors include:

- foot deformities
- calluses
- ill-fitting footwear
- limited joint mobility
- prolonged history of diabetes
- renal disease

Prevention
Diabetic ulcer prevention begins with identifying the patients at risk factors and then education to minimise or eliminate these risks, e.g. proper foot care.

Assessment
A thorough assessment of the wound and patient's history is paramount in providing the proper care and maintenance plan. Due to the complex nature of the diabetic foot ulcers and the numerous co-morbidities that can occur a multidisciplinary approach is recommended. When in doubt always refer for a team approach and support.

Wound management
Wound cleansing is key to managing the diabetic foot ulcer. Priorities for this wound are:

- aggressively treat infection
- is ischemia present
- relieve pressure
- sharp wound debridement
- appropriate dressing selection
- multidisciplinary team approach

Off-loading
Pressure reduction is a basic principle involved in the prevention of foot ulcers. Enlist the help of specialists involved in this to provide the best means of relieving pressure eg podiatrists, orthotics dept.

Complications
The most common complication of the diabetic foot ulcer is infection. This can cause the wound be become chronic and either be limb threatening or non-limb threatening. Non-limb threatening can be superficial and resolve with topical antibiotics, sharp debridement from a specialist and wound cleaning every day. Limb threatening infection involves deep tissue and bone. Surgical debridement and intervention is necessary.

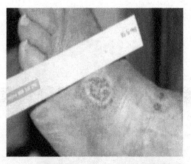

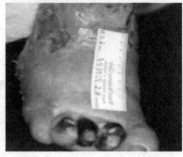

VENOUS VS ARTERIAL VS NEUROPATHIC ULCERS

Characteristics of ischemic vs venous vs neuropathic ulcers

FACTORS TO BE ASSESSED	ARTERIAL	VENOUS	NEUROPATHIC
LOCATION	Tips of toes Pressure points (e.g., heel or lateral foot) Areas of trauma (non healing wounds)	Between ankles and knees 'classic' location is malleolus	Plantar surface over metatarsal heads Areas of foot exposed to repetitive trauma (toes and sides of feet)
WOUND BED	Pale or necrotic	Dark red, 'ruddy' May be covered with fibrinous slough	Typically red (if no coexisting ischemia)
EXUDATE	Minimal	Moderate to large amounts	Moderate to large amounts
WOUND EDGES	Well-defined	Poorly defined; irregular	Well defined ; frequently associated with callous formation
OTHER	Infection common Typically painful Typically associated with other indicators: ischemia; diminished/absent pulses; elevational pallor and dependent rubor; thin fragile skin	Oedema common Hyperpigmentation surrounding skin common Feet typically warm with good pulses (if no coexisting arterial disease)	Infection common but signs and symptoms may be muted May or may not have coexisting ischemia

Pain assessment for patient with lower leg ulcer

FACTORS TO BE ASSESSED	ARTERIAL	VENOUS	NEUROPATHIC
CHARACTERISTICS	Intermittent claudication Nocturnal pain Rest pain	Dull Aching	Burning/tingling "Pins and needles" "Shooting"
SEVERITY	Variable Frequently severe	Variable Typically moderate to severe	Variable Commonly severe
EXACERBATING FACTORS	Elevation Activity Infection	Dependency Increased oedema Infection	Variable Inactivity sometimes a precipitating factor
RELIEVING FACTORS	Dependency Rest Reduction of bacterial burden	Elevation Oedema control Reduction of bacterial burden	Activity such as walking

Tables kind courtesy of: Acute & Chronic Wounds, Current Management Concepts, Third Edition. Ruth A. Bryant and Denise P. Nix

COMPRESSION
THERAPY

COMPRESSION THERAPY

COMPRESSION

Wound care clinicians treatments as temporary inconveniences until a wound is closed, but successful venous ulcer patients recognise that compression for chronic venous sufficiency (CVI) will be a necessity. This should not be interpreted as a rejection of all treatment or as disregard for the wisdom of the health care provider. Compression hosiery may be more acceptable to patients than bandaging, especially because feminine or special work footwear becomes an option when hosiery is worn. Patients are more likely to consistently wear Class II rather than Class III hosiery. Including patients in the care planning and decision making team improves venous ulcer outcomes.

Overview

Optimal graduated compression for CVI treatment is 40mmHg at the ankle, tapering to 12-18mmHg at the knee. Higher compression levels may be indicated if lymphoedema is present and lower compression levels are necessary in patients with mixed etiology wounds, including both chronic venous insufficiency and moderate arterial insufficiency. Carefully follow manufacturer's instructions when applying commercially prepared wraps. Laplace's law says the area of smaller diameter (the ankle) will experience greater pressure than the area of larger diameter (the calf) with the same amount of tension and overlap. Extra padding should be applied to uneven areas to achieve more consistent graduated compression. Compression should not extend into the smaller diameter area of the leg just below the knee, because, as Laplace's law demonstrates, this would create an area of higher pressure (reversing the gradient from what is desired).

Patients should be warned to contact the provider immediately and remove the compression if they notice numbness, tingling, increased pain or dusky toes. Injury due to inappropriate compression can lead to amputation or even death. If appropriate graduated compression leads to swelling in the thigh or groin, this indicates that the patient has significant accompanying lymphoedema, which will require specialised treatment. Patients may need to be seen twice weekly when compression is first used to assess the wound and the patient's tolerance of the compression, especially if the oedema is very painful or if the wound is highly exudating. Once the oedema is reduced, the pain and exudate should decrease and weekly changes are appropriate. Compression is contraindicated in patients with decompensated congestive heart failure or severe arterial insufficiency.

Inelastic (rigid) compression systems

Inelastic (rigid) compression systems provide relatively rigid support, giving little pressure at rest and high pressure with muscle contraction against fixed resistance. Examples are short stretch bandages, Unna's boot or modified Unna's boot. The patients' legs should be elevated or elastic bandages can be used to decrease oedema prior to initial application of inelastic compression. No compression is applied with application – graduated compression occurs when the calf muscle flexes against the rigid dressing, or when the foot pump is activated by stretching (usually with weight bearing).

Application of short stretch bandages requires training and skill. Short stretch bandages are now available with a series of hook and loop straps, simplifying application and permitting patients to remove the compression for bathing. Short stretch systems often begin at the ankle, enabling the patient to wear normal footwear. They work well with thin ankles (less than 18cm) and with oedematous feet and they are often well tolerated in patients with decreased muscle tone and significant pain. The bandages may be washed and reused several times to decrease treatment costs. Short stretch bandages tend to be much more comfortable than elastic bandages because of their low resting pressure. They are suitable for patients with ABPI >0.8 and 1.2. After the patient's oedema and pain levels have decreased using short stretch bandaging, it is possible multi-layer elastic bandaging will then be tolerated.

Elastic compression systems

Elastic compression systems have high pressure at rest and somewhat less pressure with muscle contraction. More significant CVI requires increased graduated compression. Multi-layer wraps, tubular compression devices and USA Class III hosiery all provide high-level graduated elastic compression (40mmHg at the ankle, 17mmHg at the knee), which increases healing rates. Compression at these levels increases the blood flow velocity and reduces oedema. Four-layer wraps tend to be bulky. Multi-layer bandages are intended for use in patients with ankle circumferences between 18cm and 26cm measured at 2.5cm superior to the medial malleolus. They must be correctly applied to provide the appropriate level of compression. An additional layer of the third component can be added to four-layer wraps for ankles of larger diameters to increase the total amount of compression. Not all patients can tolerate four-layer wraps.

Compression hosiery

Graduated compression stockings (hosiery) are recommended as maintenance therapy to prevent ulcers. These stockings can be expensive, so they are not usually recommended for initial compression because a custom fit is required and as the oedema decreases, the size needed will change. Legs must be measured individually, since on some patients the size differences between limbs may be significant. Compression hosiery may need to be custom-made in patients with significant lower leg deformity from venous disease. Thigh-high hosiery has not been found to be superior to knee high for CVI unless the leg has a deformity. Stockings do not always provide the graduated compression the labels claim they will give.

Advise patients not to fold the stocking over at the top, as having two layers increases compression. Two pairs of stockings should be purchased so that one can be handwashed and air-dried while the other is worn. Stockings lose stretch through use, so they should be replaced every 3–6 months. Stockings should be removed before bathing at night and be replaced

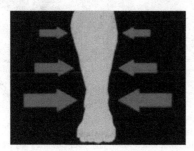

A bandage applied with constant tension will automatically provide graduated compression on a leg of normal dimensions with the highest pressure applied at the ankle.

COMPRESSION THERAPY CONTINUED

in the morning before the patient rises from the bed (before oedema has a chance to develop). Apply non-sensitizing, 24-hour moisturiser after bathing to be absorbed by the skin during the night to prevent itching from dryness. Ankle and knee flexion exercises are advisable even with the use of graduated compression stockings.

Graduated compression stockings may be very difficult to put on. Applying a silk bootee or other device first to decrease friction, or using a frame over which the stocking is stretched may help. Stockings with zippers and two piece stockings (separate foot and leg pieces that overlap at the ankle) are also available. Two layers of Class I hosiery produce higher resting pressures than a single class III stocking and may be easier to put on. Another option is a low compression liner with a higher compression overstocking. In either case, the patient can take the outer stocking off at night. The patient may, however, find the increase in stiffness caused by the friction between the two layers to be unacceptable. Orthotic compression devices using Velcro are another option.

Hosiery alternatives
Single-layer elastic (long-stretch) wraps do not provide graduated compression and are not recommended. Antiembolic stockings and standard support hose are not appropriate for patients with CVI. Multilayer bandaging systems more effectively maintain the leg's volume. In general, high and multi-layer compression is more effective than lower compression or single layer wraps. Patients with a significant arterial component to their disease (ABPI<0.8) must use modified levels of compression. But, the most supportive compression the patient will tolerate should be applied consistently when treating venous ulcers without accompanying arterial disease.

Assessing circulatory status
It is essential to assess a venous ulcer patient's circulatory status to rule out significant arterial insufficiency prior to treatment for chronic venous insufficiencies (CVI). Arterial insufficiency usually causes the lower leg to be cold and to hurt when it is elevated, while in CVI, legs are usually warm and pain is relieved with elevation. But, mixed disease is common, and assessing a patient's ankle-brachial index (ABPI) using a hand-held Doppler is necessary prior to compression treatment for CVI.

Warning: Palpable pedal pulses are NOT proof that a patient has adequate circulation for compression, and the absence of palpable pulses does not always indicate arterial occlusion.

Evaluating a patient's ABPI
The ABPI is assessed after the patient has been supine for 15 minutes. Brachial blood pressures are taken on both arms. Then the BP cuff is placed on the leg just superior to the ankle bone and the Doppler probe (using ultrasound gel) is placed at a 45-degree angle to the dorsalis pedis or posterior tibial artery. The cuff is inflated until the Doppler signal is obliterated, then deflated slowly. When the Doppler signal returns, the number is recorded as the ankle systolic pressure. Each ankle's pressure divided by the higher of the two brachial systolic pressures gives that limb's ABPI.

Interpretation of ABPI
An ABPI of more than 1.2 indicates an invalid test due to non-compressible vessels. In older patients and patients with renal disease or diabetes mellitus, the ABPI is also unreliable due to possible arterial calcification, so, further vascular testing should be considered to rule out arterial compromise in all of

these patients. An ABPI of 1.0-1.2 is considered venous, 1.0 is considered normal and 0.8-1.0 has an arterial component. An ABPI of >0.8 indicates mixed venous and arterial insufficiency, so low compression should be used cautiously and only after further medical assessment and supervision. Patients with an ABPI of less than 0.5 should not have any type of compression and require a referral to a vascular surgeon. Arterial disease may develop over time, so ABPI's should be re-assessed every three to six months.

ABPI is calculated by dividing ankle pressure by the higher of the two brachial systolic pressures.

Doppler arterial diagnostic tool
Locating the pulses:

* dorsalis pedis - central dorsal part of foot
* posterior tibial - behind medial malleolus
* popliteal - behind the knee
* femoral - in the groin

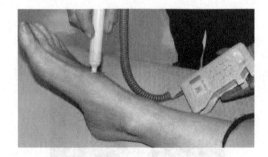

N.B. Whenever necessary, always be guided by your specialist unit when managing your patient's leg ulcer with compression therapy.

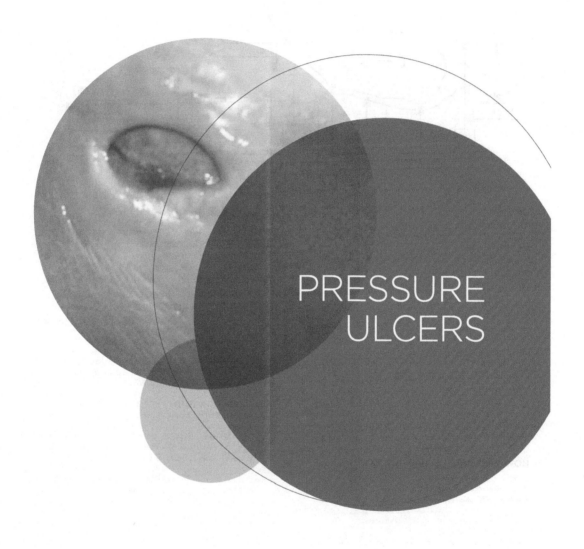

PRESSURE ULCERS

PRESSURE ULCERS

Common locations of pressure ulcers

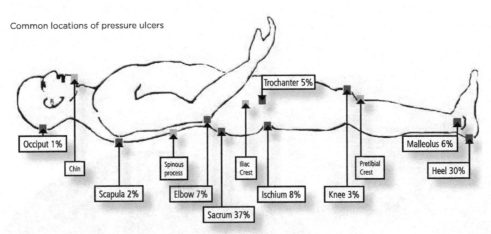

Trochanter 5%

Occiput 1%

Chin

Spinous process

Iliac Crest

Pretibial Crest

Malleolus 6%

Heel 30%

Scapula 2%

Elbow 7%

Ischium 8%

Knee 3%

Sacrum 37%

■ Indicates pressure ulcer locations with <1% frequency of occurrence

DEFINITION

Pressure ulcers are the end result of damage to the skin and/or deeper tissues caused by mechanical forces working together. According to the National Pressure Ulcer Advisory Pane (NPUAP), *"A pressure ulcer is localized injury to the skin and/or underlying tissue usually over a bony prominence, as a result of pressure, or pressure in combination with shear and/or friction."*

Pressure ulcers occur most frequently over the heaviest areas of the body. But, they can occur anywhere pressure is exerted against soft tissue by a bony prominence or a hard object (such as a tube or bedrail). Blanching erythema (redness that goes away with light finger pressure but then returns) will usually resolve completely in 2 – 3 days if it is off-loaded. It is a warning sign, but it is not a pressure ulcer. Not all open areas on or surrounding bony prominences are pressure ulcers. Moisture lesions (from incontinence associated dermatitis or excessive sweating) are not pressure ulcers, but they reduce the resiliency of the skin, which can predispose patients to pressure ulcers.

HOW PRESSURE ULCERS DEVELOP

When pressure closes off the capillaries, the surrounding tissues are deprived of oxygen and build up waste. This damages the capillary walls, causing them to leak protein. Fluid is always attracted by protein, so fluid also leaves the capillaries, causing oedema. The oedema creates additional pressure on the capillary walls which results in the capillaries closing at lower external pressures than in undamaged tissues. The worsening hypoxia and resulting damage accelerates the cellular death and inflammation.The lymph system, which usually removes excess protein from the interstitial space, is shut off by the pressure from the oedema, so the protein remains in the interstitial space, which no longer has its normal flow.This increased protein pulls fluid out of the cells, causing them to become dehydrated and irritated. When the pressure is removed, the damaged capillaries slough into the bloodstream, which may be another source of blood vessel occlusion. Pressure ulcers can develop in as little as 2 – 6 hours when normal capillary blood flow is obstructed.

Three factors determine whether or not tissue damage will occur as a result of pressure:

- intensity of the pressure (critical capillary closing pressure)
- duration of the pressure (healthy people shift their weight because tissue hypoxia causes discomfort) and
- tissue tolerance to pressure (thick, well-hydrated, healthy skin is more able to redistribute the pressure because the collagen, capillaries and fluid work together like springs).

An area of nonblanchable erythema (Stage I) usually indicates mild damage that can resolve completely with meticulous off loading. Tissue loss due to pressure damage is classified as a Stage II, III or IV pressure ulcer, depending upon the structural layer of exposed tissue.

Deep Tissue Injury (DTI)

Pressure is 3 – 5 times greater at the bone than at the skin. But, where a bony prominence is covered with muscle, the muscle distributes the load, transferring the pressure to the skin at only a small area. Muscle tissue is far more sensitive to hypoxia than skin. So, it is possible to have injury in the deep tissues without any obvious skin changes. Dark purple, with the appearance of a deep bruise is an ominous sign, often indicating Deep Tissue Injury (DTI). With DTI, if the severely damaged tissue dies, the area will open up, revealing a cavity which may extend to bone. Several studies have shown that when the deep tissues are severely injured by pressure, a visible ulcer presents about two days later.

The influence of moisture, friction and shear

Pressure is the major cause of pressure ulcers, but friction and shear can contribute, and excess moisture (or dryness) can make the skin more vulnerable to damage. Moderate increases in moisture increase friction. Friction alone causes sheet burns, not pressure ulcers. A body that is being held back by friction and is acted upon by gravity, or a dragging force, can develop deeper injuries caused by shear. Shear damages blood vessels by stretching them, rather than compressing them, and it disconnects the various levels of tissues from one another, leading to undermining in pressure ulcer-like wounds. Inflammation from shear creates intense internal pressure, so while the opening at the level of the skin may be relatively benign looking, the defect underneath tends to be quite large.

Staging

A commonly used pressure ulcer staging tool is the classification system developed by the USA based NPUAP. Over the years, this staging system has evolved, and in 2007 it was revised to clarify the four stages and to add "unstageable" and "deep tissue injury (DTI)." Current EPUAP (European) and APUAP (Australian) staging systems are very similar, although EPUAP includes DTI in the Grade IV pressure ulcer category. NPUAP created a separate category for DTI to encourage further research and to acknowledge that aggressive early interventions, including off-loading and reperfusion, may at times result in the ischemic and injured tissues being "salvaged" rather than progressing to a full thickness wound. The term "Grade" instead of "Stage" is used in Europe, but both of these terms may be replaced due to recent research. Refer to the following table for clear staging definition and descriptions of pressure ulcers.

"You can put anything on the pressure ulcer except the patient!"

TIPS FOR INDENTIFYING STAGE 1 PRESSURE ULCERS AND DEEP TISSUE INJURIES

Skill is required to distinguish between Stage I pressure ulcers and DTI, especially in patients with darkly pigmented skin. Preliminary work on a portable gauge to detect subcutaneous pressure damage shows promise, but is not yet available. To check for non-blanching erythema, apply light finger pressure for 10 seconds, release the pressure, and look for a change in skin color. A pressure ulcer is beginning to form if the skin does not lighten briefly. Warmness or coolness is present in 85% of patients with Stage I pressure ulcers. Checking for changes in skin temperature (warmer or cooler) or sensation (pain or itching) can help clinicians detect Stage I pressure ulcers on patients with darkly pigmented skin. Ultrasound can also be used to detect Stage I pressure ulcers in darkly pigmented skin. Nonblanching erythema suggests that blood has leaked into the tissues due to ischemic damage to the vessels. This must be differentiated from a Deep Tissue Injury, which is boggy or indurated (overly firm), through palpation. The discoloration of a true bruise (an injury caused by acute trauma, not prolonged pressure) extends into the epidermal layer of skin, while in pressure-related Deep Tissue Injury, the pigment of this outer layer of skin may be unaffected.

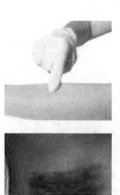

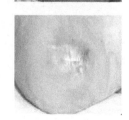

PRESSURE ULCERS

STAGING OF PRESSURE ULCERS

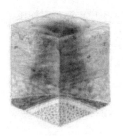 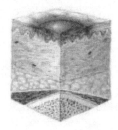 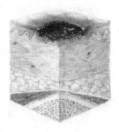

Suspected deep tissue injury
Definition: Purple or maroon localised area of discoloured intact skin or blood-filled blister due to damage of underlying soft tissue from pressure and/or shear. The area may be preceded by tissue that is painful, firm, mushy, boggy, warmer or cooler as compared to adjacent tissue.

Deep tissue injury may be difficult to detect in individuals with dark skin tones. Evolution may include a thin blister over a dark wound bed. The wound may further evolve and become covered by thin eschar. Evolution may be rapid exposing additional layers of tissue even with optimal treatment.

Stage I
Definition: Intact skin with non-blanchable redness of a localized area usually over a bony prominence. Darkly pigmented skin may not have visible blanching; its color may differ from the surrounding area.

The area may be painful, firm, soft, warmer or cooler as compared to adjacent tissue. Stage I may be difficult to detect in individuals with dark skin tones. May indicate "at risk" persons (a sign of risk).

Stage II
Definition: Partial thickness loss of dermis presenting as a shallow open ulcer with a red pink wound bed, without slough. May also present as an intact or open/ruptured serum-fi lled blister.

Presents as a shiny or dry shallow ulcer without slough or bruising.* This stage should not be used to describe skin tears, tape burns, perineal dermatitis, maceration or excoriation.

*Bruising indicates suspected deep tissue injury

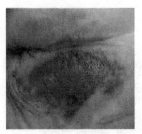 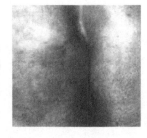 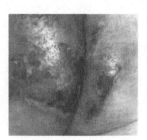

Prevention
Prevention of pressure ulcers requires two things: improving skin health to promote increased tissue tolerance and decreasing exposure to excessive pressure, friction, moisture and sheer. This can be accomplished through a formal, evidence-based pressure ulcer prevention program, which usually includes:

- a risk assessment, such as the Braden Scale Norton, Waterlow, Braden Q or similar

- a systematic skin assessment
- reducing risk factors
- patient, family and staff education and involvement
- evaluation and maintenance

It is important to note, that introducing a formal risk assessment tool linking levels of risk to prevention protocols can dramatically decrease the incidence and severity of pressure ulcers in a facility.

PRESSURE ULCERS

STAGING OF PRESSURE ULCERS CONTINUED

Stage III

Definition: Full thickness tissue loss. Subcutaneous fat may be visible but bone, tendon or muscle are not exposed. Slough may be present but does not obscure the depth of tissue loss. May include undermining and tunneling.

The depth of a stage III pressure ulcer varies by anatomical location. The bridge of the nose, ear, occiput and malleolus do not have subcutaneous tissue and stage III ulcers can be shallow. In contrast, areas of significant adiposity can develop extremely deep stage III pressure ulcers. Bone/tendon is not visible or directly palpable.

Stage IV

Definition: Full thickness tissue loss with exposed bone, tendon or muscle. Slough or eschar may be present on some parts of the wound bed. Often include undermining and tunneling.

The depth of a stage IV pressure ulcer varies by anatomical location. The bridge of the nose, ear, occiput and malleolus do not have subcutaneous tissue and these ulcers can be shallow. Stage IV ulcers can extend into muscle and/or supporting structures (e.g., fascia, tendon or joint capsule) making osteomyelitis possible. Exposed bone/tendon is visible or directly palpable.

Unstageable

Definition: Full thickness tissue loss in which the base of the ulcer is covered by slough (yellow, tan, gray, green or brown) and/or eschar (tan, brown or black) in the wound bed.

Until enough slough and/or eschar is removed to expose the base of the wound, the true depth, and therefore stage, cannot be determined. Stable (dry, adherent, intact without erythema or fluctuance) eschar on the heels serves as "the body's natural (biological) cover" and should not be removed.

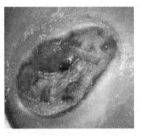  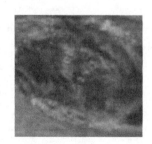

PRESSURE ULCERS

PRESSURE ULCER TREATMENT PROGRAMME

Addressing the underlying causes

The existence of a pressure ulcer should trigger the implementation of the entire prevention section of this protocol with increased intensity to prevent further damage and facilitate wound healing. Special attention should be given to

- managing incontinence and diaphoresis (excessive perspiration or sweating)
- maintaining skin hygiene and moisture
- optimising hydration and nutrition
- choosing appropriate support surfaces
- repositioning, avoiding friction and sheer

When repositioning the patient, avoid putting pressure over the area of the wound as much as possible.

ASSESSMENT

Perform an initial complete health history and physical, following up on deficits that can be corrected;

Weekly wound assessments should include:

- anatomic location of the wound
- stage or grade of the ulcer and documentation
- size in centimetres, including any tunnels or tracts with locations
- type of tissue in the wound base as a percentage of the whole
- exudate amount, consistency and type
- odour
- wound edges, or margins
- periwound condition – texture, colour, temperature, any rash
- wound pain (both persistent and incident-related)

Debridement and wound bed cleansing

Initial debridement
- do not debride wounds on patients who are terminally ill or have insufficient arterial flow for healing, such as dry stable eschar on noninfected heels. Assess these wounds daily.
- if cellulitis or sepsis is present, immediate surgical debridement of eschar and slough is indicated.
- in all other cases, use moisture-retentive dressings to cleanse the wound bed through autolytic debridement. Improvement should be seen in 72 – 96 hours.

Cleansing
- initial wound cleansing should be as thorough as the patient's condition permits.
- obvious loose wound bed debris can be removed at dressing changes. Change dressings after showering to protect the wound.
- refer for surgical debridement if appropriate

Pain management
Wound pain usually includes both persistent (background) pain and incident-related pain (from dressing changes, repositioning, debridement, etc.). New pain may indicate a developing infection.

- manage pain by eliminating the source (cover wound, adjust support surfaces, reposition patient, etc).
- when local measures are not able to eliminate or control the source of pain, analgesics should be provided as needed

Dressings
Dressings should absorb excess exudate, fill dead space, maintain moisture balance, maintain a moist wound environment, allow gaseous exchange, provide thermal insulation, protect the wound from contamination and relieve pain.

Evaluation
- evaluate pressure ulcer healing
- partial-thickness pressure ulcers (Stage I and II) should show evidence of healing within 1 – 2 weeks
- full-thickness pressure ulcers (Stage III and IV) should show a reduction in size within 2 – 4 weeks
- if the goal of care is healing and no progress is being made after two weeks of appropriate care, reassess the overall plan and look for complications, such as infection or fluid collection in the soft tissues
- refer as necessary

Infection
- local signs of infection in a chronic wound include: strong odour, purulent exudate, induration, friable or discolored granulation tissue, pocketing of the wound base, increased pain and/or delayed healing
- if a clean-appearing wound is not healing despite four weeks of optimal wound care and patient management, a two week trial of a topical antimicrobial is maybe appropriate
- a wound swab culture should be obtained if signs of infection increase
- when clinical signs of infection do not respond to treatment, osteomyelitis and joint infection should be ruled out

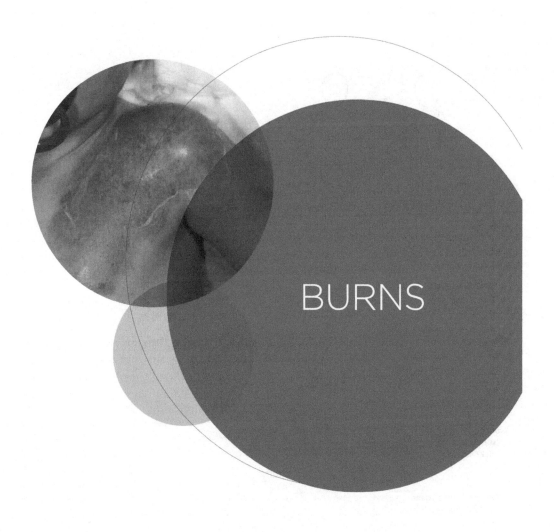

BURNS

BURNS

Estimating extent of burn injury
This is determined by The Rule of Nines which assigns a percentage to a specific body part and the total surface are then can be calculated more easily.

THE RULE OF NINES

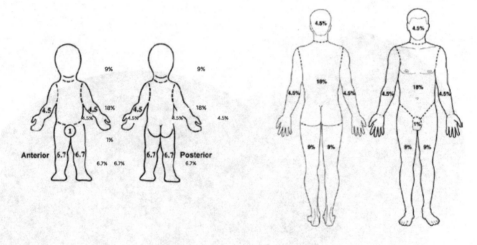

BURN SUMMARY TABLE
The following tables provides a summary of burn injuries:

Nomenclature	Layer involved	Appearance	Texture	Sensation	Time to healing	Complications
First degree	Epidermis	Redness (erythema)	Dry	Painful	1wk or less	None
Second degree (superficial partial thickness)	Extends into superficial (papillary) dermis	Red with clear blister. Blanches with pressure	Moist	Painful	2-3wks	Local infection/cellulitis
Second degree (deep partial thickness)	Extends into deep (reticular) dermis	Red-and-white with bloody blisters. Less blanching.	Moist	Painful	Weeks - may progress to third degree	Scarring, contractures (may require excision and skin grafting)
Third degree (full thickness)	Extends through entire dermis	Stiff and white/brown	Dry, leathery	Painless	Requires excision	Scarring, contractures, amputation
Fourth degree	Extends through skin, subcutaneous tissue and into underlying muscle and bone	Black; charred with eschar	Dry	Painless	Requires excision	Amputation, significant functional impairment

The Use of Polymeric Membrane Silver Dressings in Chronic Burns and Burn Related Wounds

Jacky Edwards, Clinical Nurse Specialist and Sally Ann Mason, Burns Outreach Sister
Manchester Burns Service, University Hospital of South Manchester

jacky.edwards@uhsm.nhs.uk
sally.mason@uhsm.nhs.uk

INTRODUCTION

In the past, an acute wound healing model has been applied to chronic wounds, but it is now known that chronic wound healing is different from acute wound healing[1]. Whilst it is now being recognised that chronic wounds heal differently to acute wounds and often `stick` in the inflammatory and proliferative phases, there is little or no recognition of chronicity in burn or surgical wounds. Teot & Otman[2] argue that these wounds can evolve, when poorly managed or in specific situations, into chronic wounds. Chronic burns or donor sites often continue to be managed as acute-wounds and are often dressed with conventional "burn" products. These wounds have similar problems in terms of quality of life, cost and nursing time, however little is written about this in the literature. Dressings commonly used in other chronic wounds may offer better alternatives for these burn related chronic wounds, and may allow for more continuous care when patients return to the community.

AIM

This poster sets out to evaluate polymeric membrane silver dressings on chronic burn-wounds through a prospective evaluation. A Likert-scale was used to assess pain and ease of application, pain in-situ, pain on-removal, ease of removal and acceptability of the dressings to staff and patients.

METHOD

Seven patients with ten chronic non healing burn and burn related wounds were identified. (Table1). They were treated with polymeric membrane silver dressings. These dressings have a polyurethane matrix which contains components that draw and concentrate healing substances from the body into the wound bed to promote rapid healing while facilitating autolytic debridement. The liquefied slough is absorbed by the dressing, eliminating the need for manual wound bed cleansing. The surfactant, glycerol and starch copolymer work synergistically promoting wound-cleansing and healing. The nanocrystaline silver-particles are embedded in the foam matrix and are not released onto the wound surface[3].

At each dressing change, patient comfort levels, ease of application and removal, conformability and ability to manage exudate were assessed using a 10 point Likert scale with 0 being poor and 10 being excellent. Pain levels were also measured using a 10 point Likert scale, with 0 being extreme pain and 10 being no pain. Nursing staff also documented the acceptability of the dressings.

Table 1: Demographics Chronic Burns

	Chronic Burns
Number of Patients	7 patients with 10 wounds
Mean Age	Mean Age 49 years
Male:Female Ratio	4:3
Range of duration of chronic burns	3-18 months

References

1. Dowsett, C. & Ayello, E. (2004) TIME principles of chronic wound bed preparation and treatment. British Journal of Nursing, 13:15.

2. Teot, L & Otman S (2002) Burn wound management: how to prevent a burn becoming a chronic wound. In Chronic Wound Management: The evidence for Change, Mani R (Ed). Parthenon Publishing

3. Burd A, Kwok CH, Hung SC, Chan HS, Gu H,Lam WK, Huang L. A comparative study of the cytotoxicity of silver based dressings in monolayer cell, tissue explant, and animal models. Wound Repair and Regeneration 2007;15:97-104.

4. Collier, M. (2004) Recognition and Management of wound infections. World-Wide-Wounds.

5. Foertsch, C. E., O'Hara, M. W., Stoddard, F.J., & Kealey, G. P. (1998) Treatment-resistant pain and distress during pediatric burn-dressing changes. Journal of Burn care and Rehabilitation. 19: 3: 219-24

PolyMem® Silver Wound dressing, Manufactured by Ferris Mfg Corp, Burr Ridge, IL 60527 USA. This case study was unsponsored. Ferris Mfg. Corp. contributed to this poster design and presentation.

RESULTS

The evaluations showed that the Polymeric Membrane silver dressings were easy to apply and remove, with good conformability and little or no trauma on removal.

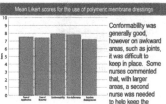

Mean Likert scores for the use of polymeric membrane dressings

Conformability was generally good, however on awkward areas, such as joints, it was difficult to keep in place. Some nurses commented that, with larger areas, a second nurse was needed to help keep the dressing in position until it was secured. These are common observations for most dressings.

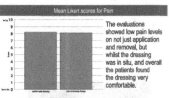

Mean Likert scores for Pain

The evaluations showed low pain levels on not just application and removal, but whilst the dressing was in situ, and overall the patients found the dressing very comfortable.

Chronic wound Healing Results

Out of the ten chronic wounds, 3 healed completely, 6 made a significant improvement and one remained unhealed. However, this wound had been present for over 18 months with no improvement from other types of dressings, and is undergoing further investigation.

Infections of Pseudomonas Aeruginosa and Staphylococus Aureus are common problems when managing burns and chronic non-healing wounds[4]. Antimicrobial dressings are used as appropriate to help minimise this problem. The polymeric membrane silver dressings performed as required, as none of the patients in these evaluations developed infections.

In the chronic group, one patient appeared to have a reaction to the adhesive, found on the border of the polymeric membrane silver oval dressing, which caused further breakdown of the wound. Following this, investigations revealed the patient had an allergy to adhesives which was previously unknown.

Feedback from the Staff

All nursing staff were happy with the product, but some nurses felt that it would be beneficial if the dressing had an adherent layer, making application easier, as it was difficult to get the polymeric membrane silver dressing to stay in place on awkward sites whilst the retention dressing was being applied in the awkward to access areas such as axilla, upper arm, buttocks etc.

DISCUSSION

This evaluation demonstrates that polymeric membrane silver dressings are a useful adjunct in the management of chronic non-healing burn-wounds. Pain is a major issue with these injuries, and it is difficult to manage[5] and can negatively impact on the patients' well-being and also on healing. It appears from the results that the Polymeric Membrane Silver dressing is beneficial in pain management. It caused minimum pain on application and removal. A number of patients experiencing pain in their wounds were included on the trial, in all cases; the patient's overall pain experience was improved.

The significant levels of exudate generally produced by these wounds can become dried and crusty on the wound surface and is painful to remove. The surfactant present in these dressings precludes this, diminishing the need for potentially painful manual wound cleansing procedures.

CONCLUSION

Polymeric Membrane dressings seem to offer good clinical advantages when used in chronic burn and burn related wounds:

- Patients reported an overall reduction in pain when using these dressings. Given that chronic wounds are painful injuries; this reduction in pain could have a positive effect on wound healing and overall return to normal function.
- Many wounds showed healing despite having been treated with numerous other dressings in the past.

Increased recognition of chronicity within Burn Care needs to be developed and as demonstrated in this initial study, products traditionally used in chronic wound management may have an advantageous place in managing the chronic burn wound. Larger sizes are needed to improve the ease of use of this product in this patient group, and we understand from the manufacturer, larger sizes are likely to be made available.

Four month old donor site. Previous treatments included various silicone and silver dressings as well as silver sulphadiazine but kept on deteriorating.

Left: Donor site after polymeric membrane silver dressings have been used for 5 weeks. 40% of the donor site is now covered with healthy granulation tissue.

Right: The donor sited closed completely after 12 weeks treatment with polymeric membrane silver dressings. The patient commented during the treatment over the reduction of pain.

Extravasation injury on a burn patient. After 2 surgical debridements followed by topical negative therapy it was still deteriorating. Photo shows the wound prior to commencing polymeric membrane dressings.

Left: Photo shows the wound after 1 weeks treatment.

Right: It closed completely three weeks later.

BURNS

A burn is a type of injury to flesh caused by heat, electricity, chemicals, light, radiation or friction. Most burns only affect the skin (epidermal tissue and dermis). Deeper tissues, such as muscle, bone, and blood vessels can also be injured. Burns may be treated with first aid, in an out-of-hospital setting, or may require more specialised treatment such as those available at specialised burn centres.

Managing burns is important because they are common, painful and can result in disfiguring and disabling scarring, amputation of affected parts or death in severe cases. Complications such as shock, infection, multiple organ dysfunction syndrome, electrolyte imbalance and respiratory distress may occur. The treatment of burns may include the removal of dead tissue (debridement), applying dressings to the wound, administering large volumes of intravenous fluids, administering antibiotics and skin grafting.

CLASSIFICATION

Burns can be classified by mechanism of injury, depth, extent and associated injuries and comorbidities.

By depth

Currently, burns are described according to the depth of injury to the dermis and are loosely classified into first, second, third and fourth degrees. Note that an alternative form of reference to burns may describe burns according to the depth of injury to the dermis.

It is often difficult to accurately determine the depth of a burn. This is especially so in the case of second degree burns, which can continue to evolve over time. As such, a second-degree partial-thickness burn can progress to a third-degree burn over time even after initial treatment. Distinguishing between the superficial-thickness burn and the partial-thickness burn is important, as the former may heal spontaneously, whereas the latter often requires surgical excision and skin grafting.

CLASSIFICATION OF BURNS

Epidermal burn (first-degree)
- erythematous, pink or red
- usually caused by ultraviolet radiation
- no blisters
- dry surface
- painful
- slight oedema
- spontaneous healing
- no scarring

Superficial dermal thickness burn (second-degree)
- erythematous, bright pink or red
- thin-walled blisters
- extremely painful
- moist, almost weeping surface
- moderate oedema
- spontaneous healing (14-21 days)

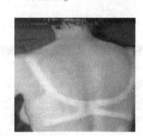

Complications

Infection is a major complication of burns. Infection is linked to impaired resistance from disruption of the skin's mechanical integrity and generalized immune suppression. The skin barrier is replaced by eschar. This moist, protein rich avascular environment encourages microbial growth. Migration of immune cells is hampered, and there is a release of intermediaries that impede the immune response. Eschar also restricts distribution of systemically administered antibiotics because of its avascularity.

By severity

In order to determine the need for referral to a specialised burn unit, the American Burn Association devised a classification system to aid in the decision-making process. Under this system, burns can be classified as major, moderate and minor. This is assessed based on a number of factors, including total body surface area (TBSA) burnt, the involvement of specific anatomical zones, age of the person and associated injuries.

Wound care

Debridement cleaning and then dressings are important aspects of wound care. The wound should then be regularly re-evaluated until it is healed. In the management of first and second degree burns little quality evidence exists to determine which type of dressing should be used.

CLASSIFICATION OF BURNS

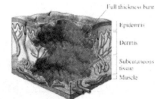

Mid dermal (second-degree)

- mixed red or waxy white
- broken blisters
- exposed surface moist
- marked oedema
- painful
- slow to heal (4-6 weeks)
- scarring

Deep dermal (third degree)

- white, yellow, brown
- poor distal circulation
- dry and rigid
- no sensation
- skin graft required
- scarring, contractures

Full thickness (fourth degree)

- charred, devitalised
- loss of function
- no sensation
- skin graft or flap required
- scarring

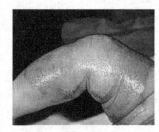
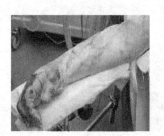
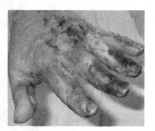

SIGNS OF INFECTION

- erythema and oedema at wound edges
- increasing pain
- odour
- drainage
- colour changes of wound
- fever

Infection can involve the depth and extent of a burn, converting a superficial partial-thickness burn into a deep partial-thickness burn.

DRESSING
CATEGORIES
AND FUNCTIONS

WOUNDCARE GUIDELINES / SUMMARY CHART

	Aim	Comments	Primary dressings include	Secondary dressings include
Black Necrotic Wound	To debride necrotic tissue if wound has potential to heal.	Careful assessment and management is important. Debridement should reveal viable tissue. Sharp debridement should only be performed by a skilled clinician	• Interactive Wet Dressing - TenderWet° Active • Hydrosorb° Gel • Purilon Gel	• For TenderWet° see "Guidelines and Expectations" Film - Hydrofilm° • Hydrogel
Yellow Sloughy - Wound Cavity	Remove slough; encourage granulation; absorb excess exudates, manage cavity.	A range of dressings will need to be combined to treat this type of wound. Generally dressings will require changing every 24-48 hours.	• Hydrosorb° Gel Interactive Wet dressing - TenderWet° Active Cavity • Calcium Alginate – Sorbalgon° • Cavity Foam - PermaFoam™ Cavity • PolyMem° Silver • Wic Rope or Cavity • SeaSorb	• Film - Hydrofilm° • Foam - PermaFoam™, PermaFoam™ Comfort • Polyacrylate sheet - Omnifix° • Relevo°
Yellow Sloughy Wound - Superficial	Remove slough; encourage granulation, absorb excess exudate.	Rehydration and exudate management.	• Hydrosorb° Gel • Interactive Wet Dressing - TenderWet° 24 Active • Hydrocolloid - Hydrocoll° • Foam - PermaFoam™ • Exudate management - Zetuvit° Plus • PolyMem° Silver • Relevo° • Comfeel° • Purilon°	• Polyacrylate Sheet fixation - Omnifix° • Relevo°
Green/Yellow Malodorous Wound	To manage odour and exudate. Assess for infection.	Careful assessment and management is important whenever infection is suspected or proven. Systemic antibiotics should be considered for infected wounds.	• Silver Dressing - Atrauman° Ag • PolyMem° Silver • Interactive wet dressing - TenderWet° active • Biatain Ag	• Exudate Management - Zetuvit° • Foam - PermaFoam™ • TenderWet° • PolyMem° silver WIC or Rope • MediHoney dressings; Antibacterial Gel, Medical Honey, Apinate and Tulle
Red Granulating Wound - Cavity Wound	To protect granulating tissue; encourage epithelialisation; absorb excess exudate; provide a moist wound environment.	It is important to select a dressing that absorbs exudate but does not place excess pressure on the healing tissue.	• Interactive Wet dressing - TenderWet° Active Cavity • Calcium Alginate -Sorbalgon - sheet or rope • Cavity Foam - PermaFoam™ Cavity • PolyMem° Cavity	• PermaFoam™ Adhesive • Exudate Management - Zetuvit° • Polyacrylate Sheet - Omnifix° • Peha-Haft° if located on limb etc • Relevo°
Red Granulating Wound	To protect granulating tissue; encourage epithelialisation; absorb excess exudate; provide a moist wound environment.	Exudate levels can vary. Depending on the choice of dressing and the exudate level, wounds can be dressed every 1-7 days.	• Hydrocolloid - Hydrocoll° • Foam -PermaFoam™, PermaFoam™ Comfort • PolyMem°	• Polyacrylate fixation sheet - Omnifix° • Film - Hydrofilm°
Pink Epithelialising Wound	To protect and promote epithelialisation.	Epithelialising minimal Wounds normally only produce minimal exudate. Depending on dressing choice wounds can be dressed every 3-7 days.	• Hydrogel sheet - AquaClear • Hydrocolloid - Hydrocoll°, Hydrocoll° Thin • Film - Hydrofilm°, Hydrofilm° Plus	• Films -Omnifix°

N.B. These recommendations are a guide only as proper wound and patient assessment should be conducted as to appropriate dressing selection and use.

WOUND ASSESSMENT TOOLS

OBJECTIVE		WOUND TYPE	
WOUND BED PREPARATION	Remove nectrotic tissue	Necrotic	
		Sloughy	
	Remove bioburden	Infected	
	Manage exudate		
SUPPORT AND PROTECTION	Support granulation	Granulating	
	Support epithelialisation	Epithelialising	

	ACTION	DRESSING CHOICE
Black cap - soft or hard eschar *Aim: Rehydrate and debride, manage exudate*	Debride necrotic tissue	Debriding agent
	Manage cavity wounds	Cavity Dressing
Yellow/greyish devitalised tissue *Aim: Remove slough, encourage granulation and manage exudate*	Remove dry, sloughy, fibrinous tissue	Debriding agent
	Manage bacterial colonisation	Silver anti-microbial agent
Green. High exudate *Aim: Manage infection and exudate*	Remove purulent exudate	Absorbent dressing
	Continue management of bacterial colonisation	Silver anti-microbial agent
	Absorb excess exudate	Exudate management agent
Red granulating tissue **Light to moderate exudate** *Aim: support and protect granulation, manage exudate*	Manage exudating wounds	Absorbent dressing
	Manage bacterial colonisation	Silver anti-microbial agent
	Manage cavity wounds	Cavity Dressing
	Support mature granulation tissue	Moist wound dressing
Epithelial tissue **Minimal exudate** *Aim: Provide hydration and protection*	Maintain moisture	Moist wound dressing

WHAT DRESSING FOR WHAT WOUND?

APPROPRIATE DRESSING SELECTION AND APPLICATION CHART

Name	Generic specifications	Dressing products/ranges	Advantages	Disadvantages
HYDROGEL **Amorphous Gels** Please note: manufacturer's recommendation for storage and single use application Exudate Capacity: Nil - low	Colloids consisting of polymers that expand in water, but are insoluable. Available in gels, sheets, or hydrogel impregnated dressings	Hydrosorb' Gel - HARTMANN Purilon' - COLOPLAST	Provides moist wound environment for cell migration Reduces pain, keeps nerve endings moist Re-hydrates eschar, autolytic debriding Easily irrigated	Gel will require secondary dressing May macerate surrounding skin with liberal use Some patients may experience a sensitivity to the preservative agents
HYDROGEL GEL SHEET Exudate Capacity: Nil - low	Dressings can be left up to 5-7 days, subject to exudate	Hydrosorb' Gel Sheet HARTMANN Medihoney HCS - DERMA SCIENCES	May not require secondary dressing Can remain in-situ for up to 7 days Allows for easy wound inspection through the dressing	Should not be used on infected wounds
HYDROCOLLOID Exudate Capacity: Low - moderate	Incorporate hydroactive or hydrophillic particles bound to a hydrophobic polymer Moisture retentive dressing as the hydrophillic particles absorb moisture and converts to a gel at the wound interface. Polymer outer layer of the adhesive hydrocolloid dressing is either semi-occlusive or occlusive **Dressing frequency:** May be left intact for up to 5 - 7 days, subject to the amount of exudate (a week, or a leak)	Hydrocoll' - HARTMANN Comfeel' - COLOPLAST	Hydroactive particles absorb exudate Gel formation at wound surface provides moist wound environment. Waterproof and bacteria proof, allows patient to shower Conforms to wound surface Hydrocolloid interaction cleans and debrides by autolysis Safe debridement, granulation and epithelisation can occur in the wound at the same time Can be used with hydrocolloid pastes and powders, for greater absorbency and reduction of dead space in the wound	Deep wounds require a cavity filling paste Edges may roll Difficult to keep in place if affected by friction - may require taping Not recommended on wounds clinically infected

Name	Generic specifications	Dressing products/ranges	Advantages	Disadvantages
CALCIUM ALGINATE Exudate Capacity: Moderate - high N.B Do not use on dry wounds, or wet, prior to use	Natural polysacchiride from seaweed Various sizes, ribbons and ropes **Dressing frequency:** Up to 5 days subject to the amount of exudate	Sorbalgon* - HARTMANN SeaSorb - COLOPLAST	Active ion exchange at wound surface forms soluble sodium alginate that provides a moist wound environment May be used to pack sinuses and cavities in order to reduce dead space in wounds Absorbent - useful in exudating wounds Promotes haemostasis in bleeding wounds Low allergenic	Alginates attached to semipermeable or occlusive dressing are not recommended for anaerobic infected wounds Gels may be confused with pus or slough Not suitable for dry wounds or in presence of hardened eschar
FOAM PolyMem® Exudate Capacity: Moderate - High Biatain® Exudate Capacity: Moderate - High Perma Foam® Exudate Capacity: Moderate	Polyurethane foam dressing in sheets or cavity filling shapes. Some incorporate a semipermeable, waterproof, adhesive layer as an outer layer of the dressing **Dressing frequency:** Up to 4-5 days, subject to the amount of exudate	PermaFoam*- HARTMANN PolyMem* Ferris Biatain*- COLOPLAST	Available as non-adherent and adherent dressings Facilitates a moist wound environment Absorbent Provides protection FOAM CAVITY DRESSINGS: reduce dead space in wounds; conform to cavity shape, absorb large amounts of exudate, reducing the need for frequent dressing changes	Moist wound environment may not be sufficient to allow autolysis to occur
EXUDATE MANAGEMENT Exudate Capacity: Moderate - High	A super absorbent polymer dressing for heavily exudating wounds **Dressing frequency:** Change when the dressing saturates depending on the level of the exudate	Relevo* Zetuvit* Plus	Designed specifically to absorb high levels of exudate Doesn't leak Can be used under compression	Shouldn't be used with film dressing May cause maceration if dressing not changed frequently enough
INTERACTIVE WET THERAPY DRESSINGS Exudate Capacity: Nil - High	A multi-layered dressing with a core of super absorbent polyacrylate that is pre-activated with ringers solution. This solution is continuously released from the dressing as debris is taken up into the dressing **Dressing frequency:** Daily 24 Hourly	TenderWet* 24 Active - HARTMANN TenderWet* Active Cavity - HARTMANN	Can be used on chronic, infected wounds as well as diabetic ulcers or over bone and tendon Activated ready for use Can be used on wounds with all exudate levels No contraindications	Cannot be used with occlusive dressing Requires daily dressing change Cavity dressing must have the TenderWet 24 Active placed on top of it to make it a daily dressing Peri wound area may become macerated so need to provide skin barrier protection Must choose appropriate size as dressing not able to be cut

WHAT DRESSING FOR WHAT WOUND?

APPROPRIATE DRESSING SELECTION AND APPLICATION CHART

Name	Generic specifications	Dressing products/ranges	Advantages	Disadvantages
Island Dressings	Primary dressing with adhesive secondary dressing	HARTMANN • Cosmopor® Advance • Cosmopor® Antibacterial • Cosmopor® E • Cosmopor® Steril 	Suitable for wounds healing by primary intention and low exudate Some have a water resistant outer layer	Not suitable for high exudating wounds Not recommended for allergies to adhesive agents
Non Adherent Dressings	Thin perforated polyester film or non-stick agent, attached or bonded to a cotton and/or acrylic absorbent pad. Non adherent surface may be single or double sided. Non-adherent dry dressings are frequently used as the contact layer in island dressings **Dressing frequency:** Left intact for up to 5 days, subject to the amount of exudate	Interpose 	Suitable for epidermal wounds, healing by primary intention Low adherence film prevents shedding of fibres into wounds	Not suitable for highly exudating wounds Dressing may dry out and stick, leading to traumatic removal of the dressing
Semi-permeable Film	Adhesive, thin transparent polyurethane film Also available as an island dressing with a low adherent pad attached to the film **Dressing frequency:** Every 5-7 days, subject to the amount of exudate	HARTMANN • Hydrofilm® 	Permeable to gases Allows some moisture vapour to be evaporated from wound Impermeable to liquids and bacteria, whilst showering Reduces pain, keeps nerve endings moist Allows inspection of wound through the dressing	Non-absorbent, exudate may pool at wound site causing maceration Not suitable for moderate to highly exudating wounds If not correctly removed may be traumatic to tissue
Medihoney Range	Antibacterial products for topical use in chronic and acute wounds	• DERMA SCIENCES Medihoney™ 	Very effective against bacteria Fast effective autolytic debridement Removes malodours Wide range of applications available	May cause slight stinging on application

Name	Generic specifications	Dressing products/ranges	Advantages	Disadvantages
Silver Dressings	**Dressing frequency:** Depends on the amount of exudate and the type of silver dressing applied	HARTMANN • Atrauman˚ Ag • FERRIS • PolyMem˚ • COLOPLAST˚ • Biatain˚ Ag 	Prepares the wound bed for healing Can leave intact and just change secondary dressing	Requires the wound to be moderately exudating to be effective to activate the silver Usually requires a secondary dressing Should be used for short periods and regularly assessed
Film Island Dressings	Primary dressing with an adhesive film secondary dressing	HARTMANN • Hydrofilm˚ Plus	Waterproof Bacteria proof	Not recommended for clinically infected wounds
Wound Contact Layer Dressings	Close weave tulle dressings, impregnated with triglyceride or petroleum jelly	HARTMANN • Atrauman˚	No fibres shed into the wound Able to stay in-situ whilst outer dressing is changed Can be used as a wound contact layer under compression	

WOUNDCARE
PRODUCTS

USL WOUNDCARE PRODUCTS

REMOVE NECROTIC TISSUE
- Hydrosorb* Gel
- TenderWet* 24 Active and Cavity
- Purilon Gel

REMOVE BIOBURDEN
- Comvita MediHoney™ Range
- Sorbalgon* and Sorbalgon* T
- Atrauman* Ag
- PolyMem* Silver
- SeaSorb
- Biatain Ag
- Cosmopor Antibacterial

MANAGE EXUDATE
- Relevo*
- Zetuvit* Plus
- PolyMax*
- PermaFoam*
- Biatain

SUPPORT GRANULATION
- Atrauman*
- Hydrosorb Gel Sheet*
- Hydrocoll* and Hydrocoll* Thin
- PolyMem*
- Biatain*
- Comfeel*

SUPPORT EPITHELIALISATION
- Hydrosorb Gel Sheet*
- Hydrocoll* Thin
- Cosmopor* E and Cosmopor* Advance
- Comfeel
- Hydrofilm* and Hydrofilm* Plus
- Zetuvit*

SKIN CLOSURE
- Omnistrip*

SKIN INTEGRITY & PROTECTION
- Niltac™
- Silesse™
- Cavilon™
- SKIN-PREP* and NO-STING SKIN-PREP*
- REMOVE*

RETENTION/FIXATION
- Omnistrip*
- PehaHaft*
- Lastotel*
- Omnifix*
- Tegaderm*
- OpSite*

NEGATIVE PRESSURE WOUND THERAPY (NPWT)
- SNaP*

SCAR MANAGEMENT
- Kelo-cote*

COMPRESSION STOCKINGS
- Sigvaris*

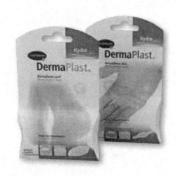

DERMAPLAST® UNIVERSAL

Air permeable and water repellent. Skin friendly – hypoallergenic adhesive.

DERMAPLAST® BLISTER

Hydrocolloid plasters offer the prevention and treatment of blisters. DermaPlast® relieves pressure and pain, is highly comfortable and skin compatible. Protects against water, dirt and bacteria.

DermaPlast® Universal

Code	Size	Unit
7307	Assorted	40/box
9099	Assorted	20/box

DermaPlast® Blister

Code	Size	Unit
7300	Small	8/box
7301	Large	6/box

DERMAPLAST® TEXTILE

Air permeable. Elastic and snug fitting Skin friendly – hypoallergenic adhesive.

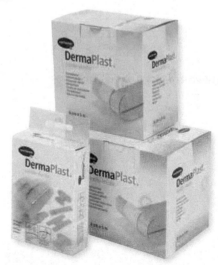

DermaPlast® Textile

Code	Size	Unit
8984	Assorted	16/box
7304	Assorted	20/box
1278	6cm x 10cm	10/box
1279	8cm x 10cm	10/box
1280	6cm x 5m	box
1281	8cm x 5m	box

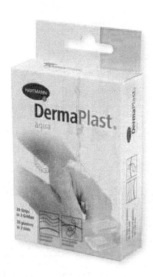

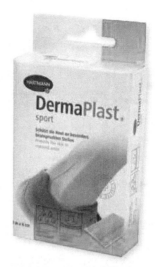

DERMAPLAST® AQUA

Totally waterproof and breathable.
Skin friendly – hypoallergenic adhesive.

DERMAPLAST® SPORT

Air permeable, cushioned protection.Water resistant and dirt
repellent. Skin friendly.

DermaPlast® Aqua

Code	Size	Unit
8983	30 x 40mm and 40 x 60mm	20/box

DermaPlast® Sport

Code	Size	Unit
9101	6cm x 10cm	10/box

USL UNIVERSAL PLASTIC AND FABRIC PLASTERS

Plastic
- everyday protection
- hypoallergenic adhesive
- water and dirt resistant

Fabric
- extra thick
- everyday protection
- superior elastic fabric

USL Universal Plastic Plasters

Code	Size	Unit
9763	19mm x 72mm	100/box

USL Universal Fabric Plasters

Code	Size	Unit
9764	19mm x 72mm	100/box

MEDICOMP®

Medicomp® non-woven swabs may be used as an alternative to traditional gauze swabs in many clinical settings on the ward and in outpatient treatment.

Medicomp® non-woven swabs, made of 66% viscose and 34% polyester fibres, have an open, gauze-like structure. They are very absorbent, soft and permeable to air.

The fabric is bonded mechanically and does not contain binding agents or optical brighteners.

Medicomp® non-woven swabs are available in a variety of sizes and piles, sterilised for immediate use and in a non-sterile presentation.

KOMPRESSEN®

Kompressen® is an unsterile cotton gauze which may be used in a variety of clinical settings.

Kompressen® swabs are available in a variety of sizes in a non-sterile presentation.

Medicomp®

Code	Size	Unit
1265	10 x 10cm, 4ply	100/pkt
1263	5 x 5cm, 4ply	100/pkt
1264	7.5 x 7.5cm, 4ply	100/pkt

Kompressen®

Code	Size	Unit
1254	10 x 10cm, 12 ply	100/pkt
1252	5 x 5cm, 12 ply	100/pkt
1253	7.5 x 7.5cm, 12 ply	100/pkt

ZETUVIT®

An absorbent dressing pad specifically developed for light-moderately exudating wounds

Zetuvit® is a multi-layered exudate management dressing pad. It is soft, comfortable, cost effective and can be used under compression bandages.

Zetuvit® is covered in a soft, non-woven, hydrophobic polyamide fibre. The inner surface of the cover has a high capillary activity, providing wicking of wound exudate into the central core of cellulose fluff.

The bleached cellulose tissue layer rapidly disperses fluid to maximise the use of the central absorbent layer.

The backing layer of hydrophobic cellulose is permeable to air and is moisture-repellent to help prevent strike-through.

Zetuvit® can be used to manage light-moderately exudating wounds and as a primary dressing on surgical wounds.

Zetuvit® Sterile, individually sealed

Code	Size	Unit
1255	10 x 10cm	25/box
1256	10 x 20cm	25/box
1257	20 x 20cm	15/box

ATRAUMAN®

A low adherent primary contact layer

Atrauman® is a low adherent, fine-weave, primary contact layer, impregnated with a non-medicated, non-petroleum based triglyceride for atraumatic wound treatment.

The soft, thin support material of Atrauman® is made of polyester and ensures close contact with the whole surface of the wound, allowing an easy passage for exudate and reducing the risk of maceration.

The fine weave and hydrophobic surface of Atrauman® counteracts adhesion to the wound by helping to prevent new tissue from penetrating the dressing. This is further enhanced by the triglyceride, which keeps the wound edges soft and supple.

Atrauman® can be combined with numerous secondary dressings including Zetuvit® and Zetuvit® Plus, PermaFoam™ for wounds requiring excessive exudate management.

Indications:

- abrasions and lacerations
- leg ulcers
- pressure ulcers
- burns and scalds
- skin graft sites
- nail extraction or wedge resection

ATRAUMAN® Ag SILVER

Versatile, economic, low adherent triglyceride impregnated silver dressing

Atrauman® Ag is a low adherent, wound contact layer dressing which contains silver. The dressing consists of a soft, thin polyamide fabric which is chemically bound with metallic silver.

The silver tulle is coated with a non-petroleum, triglyceride based ointment. The triglyceride based ointment creates a hydrophobic surface enhancing the dressing's low adherent properties, therefore protecting, caring and nourishing the peri-wound area.

When in direct contact with wound exudate, Atrauman® Ag forms silver ions on its metallic surface. The silver ions are kept within the dressing where they bind to and destroy a broad spectrum of bacteria.

The wound exudate together with the dead bacteria and endotoxins, pass easily through the dressing's fine weave and are absorbed and retained in the secondary dressing. Removal of the bioburden into the secondary dressing helps with wound bed preparation and reduces the risk of maceration.

With these characteristics Atrauman® Ag manages contaminated, traumatic wounds, helping to reduce the risk of bacterial colonisation. Atrauman® Ag is effective against a wide spectrum of bacteria including gram positive and gram negative bacteria and is suitable for use in chronic wounds of various aetiologies.

It is contraindicated for full thickness burns and wounds that are non exudating.

Atrauman® Ag can be used with a variety of secondary dressings depending on the wound requirements. For highly exudating wounds, it can be used in combination with Zetuvit® Plus.

Atrauman® Ag can remain on a wound for up to 3-4 days depending on clinical assessment.

Atrauman® Ag Silver Sterile, individually sealed

Code	Size	Unit
8903	5 x 5cm	3/box
8904	5 x 5cm	10/box
8905	10 x 10cm	3/box
8906	10 x 10cm	10/box
8907	10 x 20cm	3/box
8908	10 x 20cm	10/box

Atrauman® Sterile, individually sealed

Code	Size	Unit
1413	5 x 5cm	10/box
7366	5 x 5cm	50/box
1414	7.5 x 10cm	10/box
7367	7.5 x 10cm	50/box

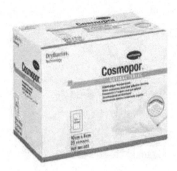

COSMOPOR® ANTIBACTERIAL

Cosmopor Antibacterial with integrated silver layer

Cosmopor Antibacterial is a sterile, adhesive wound dressing containing silver, which provides additional infection prophylaxis.

Cosmopor Antibacterial has an additional layer of silver which is located between the transfer layer and the absorption layer.

It releases silver ions within the wound pad, when activated by the moist environment. Laboratory tests show that the silver ions destroy bacteria in the wound pad, and thus minimize the risk of infection.

Cosmopor® Antibacterial Sterile, individually sealed

Code	Size	Unit
13665	7.2x5cm	25/pkt
13666	10x6cm	25/pkt
13667	15x6cm	25/pkt
13668	10x8cm	25/pkt
13669	15x8cm	25/pkt
13670	20x10cm	25/pkt

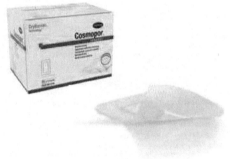

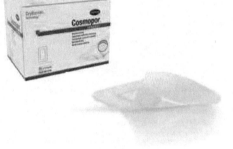

COSMOPOR® ADVANCE

A sterile, self adhesive island dressing

Cosmopor® Advance is a self-adhesive wound dressing that is ideal for post-operative wound management.

The pad is made with 100% pure cotton, allowing it to conform to the body's contours and provide cushioning.

The pad and surface layer are mounted on a soft, non-woven support that is permeable to air. Cosmopor® Advance is covered with a special low adherent layer that helps prevent adherence to the wound.

Cosmopor® Advance has a wide, continuous polyacrylate adhesive border. This ensures good closure and protection against contamination, as well as being a low irritant to the skin.

Cosmopor® Advance Steril Sterile, individually sealed

Code	Size	Unit
1302A	10x6cm	25/pkt
1304A	10x8cm	25/pkt
1305A	15x8cm	25/pkt
1301A	7.2x5cm	25/pkt

COSMOPOR® E STERIL

A sterile, self adhesive island dressing

Cosmopor® E Steril is available as a cost-effective part of this range. This line has a viscose absorbent pad and has a colophony-free synthetic rubber based adhesive.

Cosmopor® E Steril Sterile, individually sealed

Code	Size	Unit
1432	5 x 7.2cm	50/box
1433	6 x 10cm	25/box
1435	8 x 10cm	25/box
7530	8 x 15cm	25/box
8373	10 x 20cm	25/box

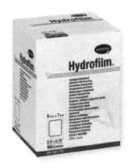
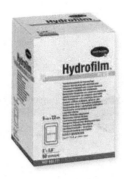

HYDROFILM®

A waterproof, transparent film dressing

Hydrofilm* is an adhesive, transparent, semi permeable, polyurethane film dressing, which is waterproof and bacteria proof.

The elasticity of the film means that the dressing conforms to the body's contours.

Hydrofilm* is used as a primary dressing to cover post operative and trauma wounds or as a secondary dressing for retention purposes.

Features:

- numbered peel off films make for easy application
- hypoallergenic adhesive layer allows initial repositioning of the film

Indications:

- post-operative wounds
- securing of catheters and cannulae
- sterile dressing for first aid
- the waterproofing of wounds

Contraindications:

- infected wounds
- over other semi-permeable dressings
- over TenderWet*

HYDROFILM® PLUS

A waterproof, transparent film dressing

Hydrofilm* Plus is an adhesive, transparent, semi permeable, polyurethane film dressing, which is waterproof and bacteria proof.

The elasticity of the film means that the dressing conforms to the body's contours.

Hydrofilm* Plus is used as a primary dressing to cover post operative and trauma wounds or as a secondary dressing for retention purposes, and features an additional absorbent wound pad.

Features:

- numbered peel off films make for easy application
- hypoallergenic adhesive layer allows initial repositioning of the film

Indications:

- post-operative wounds
- securing of catheters and cannulae
- sterile dressing for first aid
- the waterproofing of wounds

Contraindications:

- infected wounds
- over other semi-permeable dressings
- over TenderWet*

Hydrofilm*

Code	Size	Unit
1090	6 x 7cm	10/box
1081	6 x 7cm	100/box
1091	10 x 12.5cm	10/box
1082	10 x 12.5cm	100/box
1420A	10 x 15cm	50/box
1082	10 x 15cm	50/box
1084	15 x 20cm	50/box
1083	12 x 25cm	25/box

Hydrofilm* Plus

Code	Size	Unit
1421	5 x 7.2cm	50/box
1086	9 x 10cm	50/box
1087	9 x 15cm	5/box
1088	10 x 20cm	25/box
1080	10 x 30cm	25/box

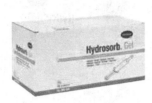

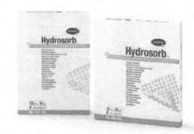

HYDROSORB® GEL

Preservative-free hydrogel in convenient application

Hydrosorb° Gel is a clear, viscous, sterile gel which is used for the treatment of dry chronic wounds. It contains Ringers solution, glycerol, hydroxy-ethyl cellulose, carboxy-methyl cellulose. It does not contain polyethylene glycol.

Hydrosorb° Gel provides a moist wound environment helping to promote wound healing. It softens dry necrotic tissue, while facilitating the removal of devitalised tissue and absorbing wound debris and exudate.

The syringe presentation enables gel application to be delivered directly into the wound for safe, clean dosing. The reverse scale plunger allows accurate measuring of dispelled contents to the nearest millimetre, thus minimising the risk of application errors and enabling simple documentation.

The gel may be left on a wound for up to three days depending on wound and requires a suitable secondary dressing to prevent drying out, e.g. Hydrofilm°.

Indications:
- rehydration and debridement of slough and necrotic tissue
- to provide a moist environment in wounds of various aetiology
- pain relief

Contraindications:
- full thickness burns

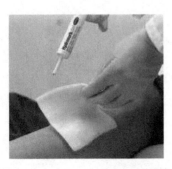

Hydrosorb° Gel

Code	Size	Unit
11205	8g	5/box
1048	15g	each

HYDROSORB® GEL SHEET

A transparent, solid hydrogel sheet that supports granulation and epithelialisation

Hydrosorb Gel Sheet® is a transparent, solid hydrogel sheet dressing with a semi-permeable outer layer.

The dressing's 60% water content makes it particularly effective for stimulating tissue growth by keeping the young epithelium and granulation tissue moist.

The soft elastic property of Hydrosorb Gel Sheet® creates a cushioning effect, which provides protection to the wound. It has a soothing and cooling effect on superficial burns and minor skin irritations.

Hydrosorb Gel Sheet® does not adhere to the wound, and can be removed without pain or disturbance to the wound bed. For nil to low exudating wounds, Hydrosorb Gel Sheet® can stay on the wound for up to seven days, making it a very cost-effective dressing.

Wound tracing film backing:

Hydrosorb Gel Sheet® has a 'write on' removable transparent film for wound tracing. This peel off film can be placed in the patients' notes for monitoring wound progress.

Indications:
- leg ulcers and pressure ulcers
- superficial or partial thickness burns
- pain management in arterial leg ulcers
- abrasions

Contraindications:
- wounds with moderate to high exudate
- infected wounds

Hydrosorb®Gel Sheet is available in two forms – Hydrosorb®Gel Sheet and Hydrosorb®Gel Sheet Adhesive. Hydrosorb®Gel Sheet will require a retention tape or bandage while Hydrosorb®Gel Sheet Adhesive features its own adhesive film border.

Hydrosorb° Gel Sheet   Hydrosorb° Gel Sheet Adhesive

Hydrosorb® Gel Sheet

Code	Size	Unit
13179	5 x 7.5cm	5/box
13180	10 x 10cm	5/box

Hydrosorb® Gel Sheet Adhesive

Code	Size	Unit
13181	7.5 x 10cm	5/box
13182	12.5 x 12.5cm	5/box

SORBALGON®

A supple, absorbent, soft-gelling alginate dressing

Sorbalgon® is a soft gelling alginate dressing composed of textile fibres of calcium alginate. It is a highly conformable dressing ideal for managing cavity wounds.

When Sorbalgon® comes into contact with the wound exudate or blood, a gel is formed by the exchange of calcium ions in the dressing for the sodium ions in the wound fluid.

This gel provides a supportive, protective environment for the development of granulating tissue while managing excess exudate.

Sorbalgon® and Sorbalgon® Rope, possess a high dry and wet integrity. This results in easy handling and easy removal of the dressing from the wound since the alginate gel is less likely to disintegrate.

The dressing should be changed once it has completely turned to gel. It should not be left on the wound for more than seven consecutive days. Sorbalgon® needs to be covered with a

secondary dressing and secured with retention tape.

Sorbalgon® is highly absorbent and suitable for use on moderate to highly exudating wounds and for the effective management of cavity wounds.

Indications:

*   leg ulcers
*   traumatic wounds
*   pressure ulcers
*   fungating lesions
*   post surgical wounds

Contraindications:

*   wounds with nil or low exudate

NB Sorbalgon® should not be moistened prior to use.

Sorbalgon® Needled Dressings

Code	Size	Unit
1422A	5 x 5cm	10/box
1423A	10 x 10cm	10/box

Sorbalgon® T Rope

1448	2 g/30cm	5/box

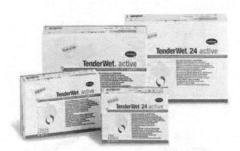

TENDERWET® 24 ACTIVE/TENDERWET® ACTIVE CAVITY

Interactive moist wound dressings that provide continuous debriding and conditioning for effective wound bed preparation

The unique properties of TenderWet® 24 Active and TenderWet® Active Cavity produce a continuous 'rinsing effect' at the wound bed, supporting effective wound bed preparation.

This multi-layered, autolytic debriding dressing comprises of:

- a central core of super absorbent polyacrylate activated with TenderWet® (Ringers) solution
- a hydrophobic cover with a high degree of conformity for direct contact with the wound bed
- a moisture-resistant top layer on TenderWet® 24 Active to enhance the 24 hour action and prevent strike-through of TenderWet® solution and exudate

TenderWet® 24 Active and TenderWet® Active Cavity are the ideal dressings for wounds requiring wound bed preparation including debridement.

Indications:

- necrotic, sloughy wounds
- infected wounds
- dehisced surgical wounds
- chronic wounds such as pressure ulcers
- leg ulcers

TenderWet® 24 Active should be changed daily. Unless used with TenderWet® 24 Active, TenderWet® Active Cavity should be changed every 12 hours. TenderWet® can be used in conjunction with a secondary dressing such as Zetuvit®/Zetuvit® Plus, then fixed into place with a bandage or Omnifix®.

TenderWet® 24 Active and TenderWet® Active Cavity come ready-to-use. They should be used until clean granulation tissue is established. Granulating tissue can continue to be managed with Hydrocolloid dressings such as Hydrocoll®.

TenderWet® solution is displaced into the wound

Wound debris and exudate is taken up into the dressing

Rinsing action provides effective debridement in an interactive moist environment

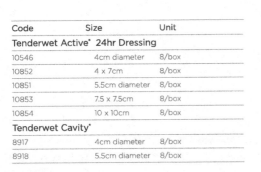

Code	Size	Unit
Tenderwet Active® 24hr Dressing		
10546	4cm diameter	8/box
10852	4 x 7cm	8/box
10851	5.5cm diameter	8/box
10853	7.5 x 7.5cm	8/box
10854	10 x 10cm	8/box
Tenderwet Cavity®		
8917	4cm diameter	8/box
8918	5.5cm diameter	8/box

SssN.B. TenderWet® guidelines for use must be adhered to for appropriate wound healing outcomes. Please ask for your copy.

CASE STUDY

Roger, an 80 year old man, was admitted to casualty with right hip pain following a fall at home five days earlier. He lives at home with his wife.

This case study is courtesy of Fleur Trezise, Clinical Nurse consultant Surgery/Wound Management.

MEDICAL HISTORY

Dementia, history of falls, hypertension, recent UTI, CABG five years ago. Roger's wife reports one episode of fever since his fall. Current medications: Ramipril, Coloxyl, aspirin, paracetamol.

EXAMINATION

Delirium secondary to sepsis, mild dehydration, constipation. No hip fracture on X-ray.

WCC:	13.6 on admission
ESR:	127
CRP:	280
Albumin:	30
Protein:	70

WOUND PROFILE

Multiple pressure sores over right hip with surrounding cellulitis.

Wound swab:	Mixed growth + coliform, ++ skin flora
Wound bed:	Necrotic
Grade:	Grade IV pressure ulcer (ascertained post debridement)
Wound measurement:	8cm x 7cm
Wound depth:	Not obtainable at initial assessment
Peri-wound skin:	Cellulitis, erythematous
Wound exudate:	Nil
Wound odour:	Offensive

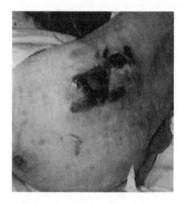

Prior to treatment necrotic burden evident.

MANAGEMENT

The wound was not suitable for surgical intervention, so conservative management with TenderWet® 24 Active was commenced. We chose to use TenderWet® 24 Active because we wanted rapid cleansing and debridement of the wound, and it's an ideal dressing for these situations. The patient was also treated with IV flucloxacillin, dietary supplementation and oral multivitamins. The TenderWet® 24 Active dressing was changed daily, and after seven days the necrotic tissue had completely softened. Sharp debridement was attended and the wound exudate was subsequently managed with a hydrofibre dressing. Once medically stable, the patient was transferred to a local nursing home with a wound plan and pressure management programme in place. Oral metronidazole, amoxycillin and multivitamins were continued following discharge.

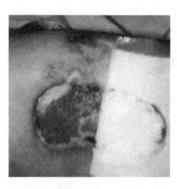

After treatment with TenderWet® 24 Active for seven days necrotic tissue completely softened.

WHY TENDERWET® ACTIVE?

TenderWet® Active was chosen for this patient not only for its rapid cleansing and debriding action, but because it was so simple for the nursing staff to use on a daily basis. TenderWet® 24 Active was covered with a combine dressing and secured in place with Hypafix tape. Each dressing remained in place for 24 hours and nursing staff commented on its ease of use.

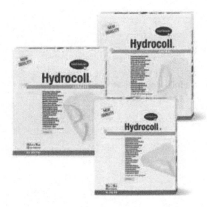
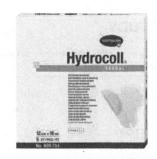

HYDROCOLL®

A thin, translucent, hydrocolloid dressing that is appropriate for all phases of wound healing

Hydrocoll® is a sterile, self adhesive, absorbent hydrocolloid wound dressing, consisting of a wound contact layer of carboxymethylcellulose hydrocolloid particles contained within an adhesive polymer matrix. The outer layer is a semi-permeable, bacteria and water proof polyurethane film.

On contact with the wound, Hydrocoll® takes up the wound exudate creating a gel. This gel provides an environment suitable for autolytic debridement, protection for granulation tissue and management of wounds of various aetiologies. Excess exudate is trapped in the upper part of the dressing and forms a blister visible on the outer layer.

Hydrocoll® is half the thickness of traditional hydrocolloids with high capacity absorbency. Its translucency allows monitoring of the wound through the dressing, while the thin, flexible material makes the dressing highly conformable.

The dressing is plasticiser-free, reducing the risk of allergic reaction.

The frequency of dressing change will depend on the wound. Hydrocoll® should be removed when there is a visible discolouration of the dressing and blister formation is about the size of the wound. Hydrocoll® can remain on the wound for 4-5 days.

Indications:
* necrotic and sloughy wounds requiring autolytic debridement
* lower leg ulcers
* pressure ulcers
* superficial and partial thickness burns
* post operative wounds
* granulating wounds

Contraindications:
* wounds with high exudate
* infected wounds
* not for use over bone or tendon
* full thickness burns
* Hydrocoll® is available in a thick and a thin version.

Hydrocoll® Thin is designed for wounds undergoing epithelialisation

Hydrocoll® Concave can be fashioned into a pocket for heel or elbow wounds

Hydrocoll® Sacral is specifically designed for pressure ulcers within the sacral region

The original and popular Hydrocoll® Sacral shape

Hydrocoll® Thin Sterile, individually sealed

Code	Size	Unit
8835	5 x 5cm	10/box
8836	7.5 x 7.5cm	10/box
8837	10 x 10cm	10/box

Hydrocoll® Sterile, individually sealed

Code	Size	Unit
8825	5 x 5cm	10/box
8826	7.5 x 7.5cm	10/box
8827	10 x 10cm	10/box
8830	15 x 15cm	10/box
8831	20 x 20cm	10/box

Hydrocoll® Sacral Sterile, individually sealed

Code	Size	Unit
8833	18 x 18cm	10/box

POLYMEM®

Not just a foam...

PolyMem® now belongs to an innovative class of adaptable multifunctional wound care dressings. PolyMem® dressings effectively cleanse, fill, absorb and moisten wounds throughout the healing continuum. No other single wound dressing combines these four key wound healing capabilities like PolyMem®.

Cleanses: Contains a mild non toxic cleansing agent activated by moisture that is gradually released into the wound bed. Built-in cleansing capabilities reduce the need to cleanse wounds during dressing changes, so you can avoid disrupting the growth of healthy tissue as the wound heals.

Fills: Gently expands to fill and conform to the wound.

Absorbs: Wicks away up to ten times its weight in exudate.

Moistens: Keeps the wound bed moist and soothes traumatised tissues, reducing wound pain and providing comfort at the wound site. The moisturiser also keeps the dressing pad from adhering to the wound so it is able to be removed virtually atraumatically.

How does PolyMem® work?

Inhibits the actions of the pain-sensing nerve endings under the dressings ("nociceptors")

These same nerves, when activated, create the series of events that result in; bruising, swelling, oedema and pain (inflammation)

Evidence suggests that the dressing might absorb sodium ions, by capillary action, from the skin and from the subcutaneous tissues

If this is true, then this local decrease in sodium ions would result in reduced nociceptor nerve conduction, which could account for the observed pain relief.

Continual cleansing

PolyMem® contains a wound-cleansing agent (F-68 surfactant) which is released into the wound when activated by moisture. This reduces the interfacial tension between healthy tissue and debris, loosens eschar and necrotic tissue, and supports autolytic debridement – all while keeping the wound bed clean during healing.

Wound comfort and health

Glycerin, a moisturiser contained in the dressing, keeps the dressing from adhering to the wound bed and provides comfort at the wound site. Glycerin also reduces odour, conserves living fat cells, reduces hypergranulation, soothes traumatised tissues and supports autolytic debridement.

Impressive wicking power

The polyurethane membrane matrix wicks away up to ten times its weight in exudate. It will not fragment and leaves no residue in the wound bed.

The superabsorbent starch co-polymer in PolyMem® absorbs and binds the water molecules from the wound fluid, allowing the

natural growth factors and nutrients to concentrate in the wound bed. Liquid barrier and gas exchange The semi-permeable thin film backing provides a liquid barrier while allowing gaseous exchange and maintaining an ideal moisture vapour transmission rate (MVTR). The transparent film backing allows for visual inspection of the membrane to determine the need for a dressing change.

Indications for use:

*   skin tears
*   pressure and diabetic ulcers
*   dermatological disorders
*   leg ulcers
*   donor and graft sites
*   surgical wounds and tube sites

Multiple configurations available for a variety of wound needs:

PolyMem®, PolyMax®, PolyMem® Silver, PolyMem® WIC (cavity dressing), PolyMem® WIC Silver (cavity dressing), PolyMem® Shapes, Oval.

Dressing protocol

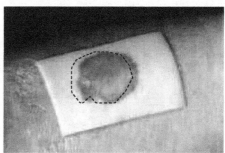

N.B. Change dressing when 75% saturated.

First time only

*   clean wound per facility protocol
*   place PolyMem® dressing on wound
*   change when exudate reaches wound margin (see above)
*   Dressing changes
*   remove old dressing (do not disturb wound bed)
*   if infected, treat accordingly
*   place new PolyMem® dressing on wound site

PAIN - THE FIFTH VITAL SIGN

*   PolyMem® dressings help reduce wound pain associated with dressing changes
*   PolyMem® dressings are completely non-adherent to the wound bed. Dressings which stick to the wound bed cause wound pain and trauma when they are removed during dressing changes and are also associated with delayed healing
*   cleansing wounds is known to cause wound pain during dressing changes. PolyMem® dressings usually eliminate the need for wound bed cleansing during dressing changes
*   PolyMem® dressings facilitate effective autolytic debridement, reducing the need for more painful debridement options

Dressing	USL Code	Description	Size	Unit
Non- Adhesive				
	10485	Non-Adhesive Pad Dressing	4.75cm x 4.75cm Pad	20/box
	8013	Non-Adhesive Pad Dressing	8cm x 8cm Pad	15/box
	8014	Non-Adhesive Pad Dressing	10cm x 10cm Pad	15/box
	8015	Non-Adhesive Pad Dressing	13cm x 13cm Pad	15/box
	8016	Non-Adhesive Pad Dressing	17cm x 19cm Pad	15/box
	8017A	Non-Adhesive Pad Dressing	10cm x 32cm Pad	each
	8018A	Non-Adhesive Roll Dressing	10cm x 61cm Roll	each
	10943	Non-Adhesive Roll Dressing	20cm x 60cm Roll	each
MAX Non-Adhesive				
	8027	MAX Non-Adhesive Pad Dressing	11cm x 11cm Pad	10/box
	90163	MAX Non-Adhesive Pad Dressing	20cm x 20cm Pad	5/box
WIC Cavity Wound Filler				
	8019	WIC Cavity Wound Filler	8cm x 8cm (4 Grams)	10/box
	8026	WIC Cavity Wound Filler	8cm x 30cm (16 Grams)	12/box
Cloth Adhesive				
	8006A	Cloth Dot Dressing	5cm x 5cm Adhesive 2.5cm x 2.5cm Pad	20/box
	8007	Cloth Island Dressing	10cm x 13cm Adhesive 5cm x 8cm Pad	15/box
Film Adhesive				
	9706	Film Dot Dressing	5cm x 5cm Adhesive 2.5cm x 2.5cm Pad	20/box
	8001	Film Island Dressing	10cm x 13cm Adhesive 5cm x 8cm Pad	15/box
	8002	Film Island Dressing	15cm x 15cm Adhesive 9cm x 9cm Pad	15/box
	8025	Film Island Dressing	10cm x 32cm Adhesive 5cm x 26cm Pad	12/box
Silver Non-Adhesive				
	1332	Silver Non-Adhesive Pad Dressing	4.7cm x 4.7cm Pad	20/box
	8029	Silver Non-Adhesive Pad Dressing	10cm x 10cm Pad	15/box
	90406	Silver Non-Adhesive Pad Dressing	17cm x 19cm Pad	15/box
	90407	Silver Non-Adhesive Pad Dressing	10cm x 32cm Pad	12/box
MAX Silver Non-Adhesive				
	9688	MAX Silver Non-Adhesive Pad Dressing	11cm x 11cm Pad	8/box
WIC Silver Cavity Wound Filler				
	1331	WIC Silver Cavity Filler	2.5cm x 7.6cm, Single Sheet	2/dressings
	8031	WIC Silver Cavity Wound Filler	8cm x 8cm (4 Grams)	10/box
	90408	WIC Silver Rope	1cm x 35cm (3 Grams)	6/box

Dressing	USL Code	Description	Size	Unit
PolyMem® Shapes - Latex Free				
	9679	#3 Oval Dressing	5cm x 7.6cm Oval Adhesive / 2.5cm x 5cm Pad	20/box
	9682	Sacral Dressing	18.4cm x 20cm Sacral Adhesive / 11.4cm x 12cm Pad	10/box
	10944	Tube Dressing	8cm x 8cm Pad	15/box
	13480	Nursicare	Sterile PolyMem Breast Pads	6/box

POLYMEM® SKIN TEARS PROTOCOL

Manage skin tears step-by-step

- Assess the cause and dimensions of the skin tear. Categorise the skin tear using the Payne-Martin Classification System
- Cleanse very gently with normal saline to remove clots and debris and rehydrate any remaining flap. Stop any bleeding with light direct pressure. Pat dry.
- Approximate edges of any remaining flap without applying tension using a few thin adhesive strips, allowing space for exudate to drain from the edge of the wound. Gently manipulate the flap using a moist cotton-tipped applicator, rather than hard instruments.
- Cover with an appropriately-sized PolyMem® or Shapes® by PolyMem® Island Dressing, or a non-adhesive PolyMem® Wound Dressing held in place with a self-adhering wrap, gauze wrap or stockinette.
- Document pain, location, size, depth, classification, treatment, teaching, and proposed prevention strategies.
- Follow-up, checking the dressing daily, or as appropriate. Leave it in place for three days unless exudate visible through the dressing reaches the approximate edge of the wound, indicating the need for an earlier dressing change. This is most common in Category IIB and III skin tears with large amounts of tissue loss. Do a routine dressing change* after three days, and then every four days until the wound is completely closed.
- Prevent recurrence by implementing the applicable changes to improve skin health and prevent trauma.

*With PolyMem® formulations, the dressing change process is simple – just remove the old dressing and place a new dressing on the wound.

- PolyMem® dressings contain a moisturizer and are non-adherent to the wound surface, assuring virtually pain-free removal and reducing the risk of disrupting healing tissues during the dressing change.
- PolyMem® absorbs up to ten times its weight in exudate, decreasing the risk of maceration.
- No wound cleansing is routinely performed during the dressing change process because PolyMem® dressings provide continuous cleansing of the wound.
- The semipermeable backing optimises oxygen and moisture vapor passage while protecting the wound from liquids and bacteria.
- Usually patients experience dramatic pain relief when PolyMem® dressings are applied. Animal studies suggest that the PolyMem® dressings interrupt the pain pathways at the wound site while enhancing healing.
- The PolyMem® formulation has also been shown in animal studies to reduce oedema and bruising while decreasing the spread of inflammation into surrounding uninjured tissues.

Always assess for pain and infection and follow-up appropriately.

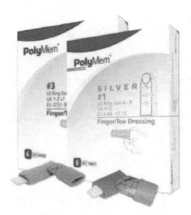

POLYMEM® FINGER/TOE DRESSING

Help improve recovery after injury

The PolyMem® Finger/Toe dressings help reduce oedema, bruising, pain and inflammation when applied to open or closed injuries. When applied to open wound the dressings continuously cleanse, fill, absorb and moisten wounds. The dressings help relieve both persistent and procedure related pain associated with the injury throughout the healing process.

The ideal choice for managing:

- sprains
- strains
- contusions
- abrasions
- lacerations
- burns
- ulcers
- matricectomies

1 Measure to determine length of dressing needed, cut off excess.

2 Remove the insert from the rolled end and discard.

3 Insert the finger into the rolled end of the dressing.

4 Push the finger into the dressing and begin rolling.

5 Roll the dressing on the finger.

6 The dressing should fit securely on finger or toe.

Dressing	Code	Description	Size	Unit
Polymem® Finger/Toe Dressings				
	11164	#1 Finger/Toe Dressing	Small	6/box
	11165	#2 Finger/Toe Dressing	Medium	6/box
	11166	#3 Finger/Toe Dressing	Large	6/box
	11167	#4 Finger/Toe Dressing	Extra Large	
	13441	#5 Finger/Toe Dressing	Extra Extra Large	
Polymem® Finger/Toe Dressings				
	11168	#1 Silver Finger/Toe Dressing	Small	6/box
	11169	#2 Silver Finger/Toe Dressing	Medium	6/box
	11170	#3 Silver Finger/Toe Dressing	Large	6/box
	11171	#4 Silver Finger/Toe Dressing	Extra Large	
	13442	#5 Silver Finger/Toe Dressing	Extra Extra Large	

CASE STUDY

Complete Pain Relief Using Polymeric Membrane Dressings* to Treat a Category III Skin Tear to Complete Closure

Lisa Ricciardo, BSN, RN, CWS, Avalon Gardens Rehab & Health Center, 7 Route 25 A, Smithtown, NY 11787

PROBLEM

A 51-year-old female long-term-care resident suffered a fall, resulting in a large hematoma to her R lateral shin. Co-morbidities included currently well-controlled diabetes with a BMI of 31.6 and HbA1c of 5.7, chronic anemia, psoriasis with long-term topical steroid use, hypothyroidism, and recent pin placement in the L leg with a secondary infection. The patient fell a second time, breaking open the area of the hematoma into a 13.0cm x 5cm x 0.1cm full-thickness skin tear. Steri-strips were applied, but the ER personnel found no salvageable flap and were unable to suture the wound. The patient was sent back to her room with antibiotic ointment and a nonadherent dressing to be changed twice a day. She was seen by the wound team the day following the second fall.

RATIONALE

Polymeric membrane dressings are proven to provide significant wound pain relief by inhibiting nociceptor activity at the wound site. They contain a gentle cleanser, so after initial debridement and/or cleaning no manual wound cleansing is usually needed, allowing for less disruption of the new growth at the wound bed and very quick and easy dressing changes. The clinician's previous experience with polymeric membrane dressings on skin tears led to the conclusion that, "it helps heal them quickly, painlessly and does help the bruising go away." Due to the patient's debilitated state and comorbidities, infection was a serious concern. Silver polymeric membrane dressings have been found effective against: *Staphylococcus aureus (MRSA and Non-MRSA), Enterococcus faecalis (VRE), Klebsiella pneumoniae, Pseudomonas aeruginosa and Candida albicans.* Recently, several other modern silver dressings were found to be severely cytotoxic in vivo, but cells in contact with silver polymeric membrane dressings proliferated. This further affirms the author's decision to use silver polymeric membrane dressings.

METHODOLOGY

The dried blood was cleansed from the wound gently with sterile water. Initially, the periwound area was swollen

OBJECTIVES

- Review evidence for the use of polymeric membrane dressings on skin tears.

- Discuss the benefits of using polymeric membrane dressings, which have been shown to help reduce wound pain not only during dressing changes, but also while the dressing is in place.

- Consider the advantages of using polymeric membrane dressings in terms of passive continuous cleansing of the wound bed, which often eliminates painful and time-consuming wound cleansing during dressing changes.

10 Jan 2006: 13cm x 5cm x 0.1cm Purulent light yellow exudate. Daily silver polymeric membrane dressings initiated. No wound pain after the first day of treatment.

17 Jan 2006: 11.5cm x 5cm Serous exudate. Changed to standard polymeric membrane dressings. The patient still states she has no wound pain at all.

30 Jan 2006: 10cm x 4.1cm No wound cleansing needed for past week. Continuing polymeric membrane dressings.

7 Feb 2006: 9.8cm x 3.1cm 95% granulation tissue. Still no pain at dressing changes or while dressing is in place.

21 Feb 2006: 5.6cm x 2.2cm 100% granulation tissue. Dressings are now being changed every other day.

21 Mar 2006: 3cm x 0.9cm 100% granulation tissue. Dressings are now being changed every third day.

4 April 2006: Closed. No wound pain during the entire time of treatment (after day 1) with polymeric membrane dressings.

...continued overleaf.

CASE STUDY CONTINUED

Complete Pain Relief Using Polymeric Membrane Dressings' to Treat a Category III Skin Tear to Complete Closure
Lisa Ricciardo, BSN, RN, CWS, Avalon Gardens Rehab & Health Center, 7 Route 25 A, Smithtown, NY 11787

with induration and the wound drained a moderate amount of purulent light yellow exudate. So, a silver polymeric membrane dressing was applied and changed daily for the first week of treatment. When the exudate was no longer purulent, standard polymeric membrane dressings were used instead. These were initially changed daily, then every other day, every three days and finally every five days. Polymeric membrane dressings were used to complete wound closure. The wound bled often during the first two weeks, so it was cleansed daily then, but it was not cleansed throughout the treatment as would have been necessary with other dressings.

RESULTS

Granulation tissue formed quickly, with complete wound closure in only three months. The patient did not have wound pain at any time after the first day, despite the depth of the wound. Slough was drawn into the dressing, revealing a clean wound bed at dressing changes. So, after the first two weeks, manual wound bed cleansing was not performed.

CONCLUSION

The polymeric membrane dressings were effective and easy to apply. After the initial cleansing and dressing of the wound by the wound team, the patient remained completely free from wound pain. The wound cleaned up quickly and healed in only three months, much faster than the clinician would have expected when using other dressings.

BIBLIOGRAPHY

1. Fleck, CA. Managing wound pain: today and in the future. Advances in Skin and Wound care 2007;20:3,138-145. 2. Hess CT. Wound Care Clinical Guide. Lippincott Williams & Wilkins. Ambler, PA. 2005; 275-6. 3. Fowler E, Papen JC. Clinical evaluation of a polymeric membrane dressing in the treatment of dermal ulcers. Ostomy/Wound Manage. 1991;35:35-38,40-44. 4. Burd A, Kwok CH, Hung SC, Chan HS, Gu H, Lam WK, Huang L. A comparative study of the cytotoxicity of silverbased dressings in monolayer cell, tissue explant, and animal models. Wound Repair and Regeneration 2007 15:94-104. 5. Beitz AJ, Newman A, Kahn AR, Ruggles T, Eikmeier L. A polymeric membrane dressing with antinociceptive properties: analysis with a rodent model of stab wound secondary hyperalgesia. J Pain. 2004 Feb;5(1):38-47.

*This case study was unsponsored. Ferris Mfg. Corp. contributed to the presentation of this poster. *PolyMem' Dressings, PolyMem Silver™ Dressings Ferris Mfg. Corp., Burr Ridge, IL 60527*

POLYMEM' DRUG-FREE DRESSINGS PROVIDE THE FOLLOWING

* significant reduction in pain
* significant reduction in the spread of the inflammatory reaction into the uninjured surrounding tissues
* significant reduction in oedema
* significant reduction in bruising
* reduced injury healing time

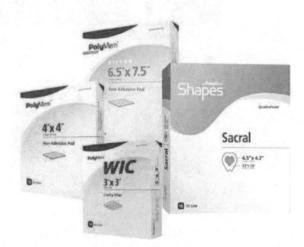

POLYMEM® SPORTSWRAP®

Get them back in the game faster

Getting your athletes back in the game is one of your main objectives. You know how important it is to control the spread of the acute inflammatory process and regain full range of motion, muscle strength and power. What you may not know is that SportsWrap® by PolyMem® has become the preferred wrap for world renowned sports medicine professionals and elite athletes.

SportsWrap® is the world's first wrap created specifically to manage athletic injuries. For you, that means quicker (more effective) management of the injury. For your athlete, that means a quicker return to game level performance.

Sports medicine professionals worldwide in professional and amateur sports are using SportsWrap®, including:

* professional sports organisations
* collegiate and high school teams
* elite athletes

HERE'S HOW IT WORKS:

Strains, sprains and contusions – where the skin is intact
Rigorous animal research studies show that SportsWrap®and PolyMem dressings inhibit the action of nociceptors, the populous raw nerve endings found in the epidermis, thereby interrupting the mechanism of inflammation and pain.

Study results revealed that, "There is robust, reproducible and statistically significant decrease in both secondary mechanical and thermal hyperalgesia" when wounds were wrapped with polymeric membrane dressings. Human case studies have

revealed dramatic reductions in oedema, ecchymosis (bruising) and pain in a wide array of athletic injuries.

SportsWrap® is nonsterile and should not be used on broken skin.

Benefits of SportsWrap® by PolyMem®

* supports the tissue, limb or joint
* cushions and helps to protect from reinjury
* helps to provide compression and stabilisation
* provides gentle counterpressure to skin surface
* is comfortably snug without restricting blood flow
* insulates from thermal and mechanical shock
* retains warmth to encourage blood flow
* protects skin from irritating stimulation and abrasion
* absorbs perspiration from skin for comfort
* moisturises, lubricates and softens skin
* long lasting, drugfree pain relief

Dressing	Code	Description	Size	Unit
SportsWrap®				
	10942	SportsWrap® (with White Fabric Over Wrap)	7cm x 40cm	6/box
	10488	SportsWrap® (with White Fabric Over Wrap)	10cm x 76cm	4/box
	10489	SportsWrap® (with White Fabric Over Wrap)	12cm x 76cm	4/box
	10487	SportsWrap® Roll	7cm x 91cm	8/box
	10490	SportsWrap® Roll	12cm x 91cm	4/box
	10491	SportsWrap® Roll	12cm x 121cm	3/box

POLYMEM® SURGICAL

- The PolyMem dressing will expand and conform to the wound
- The mild, non-ionic, non-toxic, tissue-friendly wound cleanser/surfactant and the glycerin incorporated in the dressing will be released to the wound bed/incision site, while the starch co-polymer and the foam will bind fluid in the dressing
- The semi-permeable film cover helps maintain appropriate moisture balance

PolyMem surgical has the ability to rapidly reduce inflammation, resulting in the following benefits:

Clinicians
- Improved compliance
- post-operatively
- Less chance of infection and wound breakdown
- Less reliance on analgesia
- Overall cost-benefit

Patients
- Reduced pain
- Reduced edema and swelling
- Improved rehabilitation
- overall improved clinical outcome

PolyMem® Surgical

Code	Description	Size	Unit
13437	Surgical Knee Dressing	PolyMem Surgical 13x23cm	BX5
13439	PolyMem Surgical Dressing Hip	PolyMem Surgical 14x32cm	BX5
13438	PolyMem Surgical Silver Knee	PolyMem Surgical Silver 13x23cm	BX5
13440	Surgical Hip Dressing	PolyMem Surgical Silver 14x32cm	BX5

Circumferential wrap technique with polymeric membran dressings after arthroscopic ACL reconstruction reduces blistering, inflammation and bruising; rapid recovery and improved patient satisfaction: 80 prospective patient ser

Julian Stoddart - MBChB with Distinction (Otago), FRACS (Orth) - Orthopaedic Surgeon, Adult Lower Limb Reconstruction and Sports Surgeon
New Plymouth, New Zealand

Problem

Our practice annually performs approximately 50 arthroscopic anterior cruciate ligament (ACL) reconstructions, with hamstring grafting. The sites are covered with traditional adhesive island dressings in conjunction with wool and then covered with thin wrap applied around the leg. A compressive dressing is then applied over the knee. Marked swelling and bruising often accompany these procedures. Swelling around the surgical wounds often leads to blistering under the adhesive dressings. When these blisters decompress, the risk of infection is increased. Swelling, blistering and bruising can often delay patients' rehabilitation initiation, compliance, progression, and their rapid return to normal activity and sport. These negative outcomes affect the patients' initial perception of the operation as well as making recovery more uncomfortable.

Objectives

Drug-free, multifunctional polymeric membrane dressings* (PMD) were formally evaluated because other clinicians had reported that, when placed on a surgical site, the skin and incision in contact with the PMD pad did not bruise or swell and the reduced swelling was accompanied by elimination of blistering. We had also observed these phenomena personally when using PMD dressings for hip and knee arthroplasties. Our goal was to:

- Reduce blistering and maceration associated with blister decompression.
- Reduce the spread of inflammation which results in bruising, pain and swelling; pain is recognized to slow healing and swelling is recognized to increase the risk of infection.
- Enhance inflammation resolution. This will improve patients' ability to engage in rehabilitation and reduce the risk of infection.
- Improve patients' initial rehabilitation recovery phase and ultimate return to sport and normal activity.
- Minimize surgical site infections (SSI) leading to post-operative complications.

In addition to age, gender, surgical closure detail, compliance with post-operative dressing change at 24 hours post-op and non-sterile PMD† applied, the key outcomes tracked were: swelling; bruising; pain levels at 1 and 12 days post-operatively; maceration; blistering; time to physiotherapy initiation; time to hospital discharge; average number of days to full weight bearing; days post-op full range of motion achieved; subjective patient impression.

Results

	Outcome	PMD Results Compared to Previous Approach
1.	Swelling	Reduction of swelling 30% at proximal tibial compared to previous dressing using circumference measure
2	Bruising	Marked reduction in bruising immediately adjacent to the tibial wound where PMD had been in direct contact with the skin. Less bruising tracking distally
3	Pain levels at 1 and 12 days post operatively	Pain levels similar at day 1 (as similar analgesic regime including use of local anaesthetic delivery system). At 12 days patients appeared more comfortable when compliance with use of non-sterile PMD wrap was high
4	Blistering	1 case (1.25%) of mild blistering associated with adhesive tape use. The previous dressings had blistering associated in around 15% of all the patients undergoing the surgery.
5	Maceration	Maceration eliminated. Previously maceration was a problem with the dressings used.
6	Time to self-physiotherapy initiation	Unchanged at 12 hours for PMD and original dressing group
7	Time to hospital discharge	All patients discharged after one night in hospital. Previously there was an extra night required if complications were present.
8	Average # of days to full of weight bearing	All patients discharged fully weight bearing after 1 day. With the previous dressing protocol, some patients were not able to achieve this due to the complications.
9	Days post-op full range of motion achieved	All patients (100%) flexing to at least 90 degrees by 12 days. This was not always the case with the previous dressing solution of Telfa and Wool Wrap and bandage. Only 80% were able to achieve this with the old protocol.
10.	Subjective patient impression	Marked increase in patient satisfaction at first dressing change and at 12-day mark. This increase in satisfaction appeared to lead to greater confidence in initiating rehabilitation program at the level planned.

Methods

Eighty consecutive patients undergoing arthroscopic ACL reconstruction were dressed with:

1. Intraoperative Primary Sterile Dressing Application
A. Aseptic application of 8cm x 30cm PMD cavity filler cut to cover the proximal tibial wound & medial and lateral portals.

B. Circumferential wrapping of the knee utilising sterile 20cm x 60cm PMD rolled on, without tension, in contact with the skin from the upper third of the proximal tibia to the distal third of the femur. Care taken to overlap wraps for complete skin surface cover because direct skin contact is required in order for the inflammation modulating actions to be realized.

C. Secured with a 10cm width sterile cohe Note – bandage gently applied circumferen minimal / no stretch. Goal is to assure the c in place, but not to apply compression to th purpose is to allow the dressing, without co reduce the swelling and bruising through in the contacted skin. Self-physiotherapy beg first 24 hours.

2. Postoperative Initial Dressing Change Prior to Discharge
- All intraoperative dressings removed.
- Application of PMD Film Island to the proxim
- Application of 10cm x 77cm non-sterile PMD circumferentially over the knee. This wrap to & night except for showering. If wrap becom activity, change. Patients or family members

Conclusion

Use of a PMD wound dressing protocol lead to objectively and subjectively outcomes. Bruising and swelling was noticeably reduced, particularly in the tibial region. Blistering was almost entirely eliminated. It was postulated that to reduced swelling under the PMD. Patient comfort, lack of wound problem inflammation resolution allowed an early rapid rehabilitation of the reconstru

Discussion

PMD dressings, combined with the accompanying dressing change and wi were found to be exceptional in arthroscopic ACL reconstruction with hams surgery at our hospital. The inflammatory process was concentrated on the but the surrounding tissues showed no inflammation at all. This ensured the greatly reduced chance of a post-operative infection occurring.

The patient's perception of the technical success of an operation is often cc amount of bruising, swelling and blistering. Improvement in these paramete increase the patients' confidence in the outcome of their surgery and thus p rapidly to full rehabilitation.

The dressing proved cost-effective for the hospital in terms of number of dr versus the old protocol as well as the nursing time saved in dressing chang of complications. All those factors added up to an overall cost benefit to the

Staff involved with these patients reported that the drug-free multifunctional combined with the dressing change protocols provided increased comfort f patient, improved patient compliance and participation in rehabilitation resu rapid and more cost-effective return to usual activities of daily life.

On-going commitment to the use of these dressings and dressing change p medical and nursing has been reinforced by these results, as we strive to p practice in order to continuously improve outcomes for our patients.

REFERENCES:
1.Boilz AJ, Newman A, Kahn AR, Ruggles T, Eikmeier L. A polymeric membrane dressing with antinocicept sis with a rodent model of stab wound secondary hyperalgesia. J Pain. 2004 Feb; 5(1): 38-47
2.Dawson N. Lewis C, Bock R. Total joint replacement surgical site infections eliminated by using multifunc cases report over 4 years. Poster. Australian College of Operating Room Nurses (ACORN) May 19-22, 20 Acknowledgment: T. Wolfe (Physiotherapist) provided invaluable assistance during follow-up

*PolyMem Wic, *PolyMem, †SportsWrap are manufactured by Ferris Mfg. Corp. Fort Worth, Texas 76106 USA

This case study was unsponsored. Ferris Mfg. Corp. contributed to poster design and presentation.

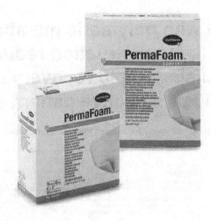

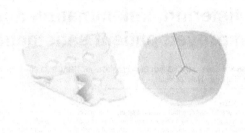

PERMAFOAM™

The absorbent, polyurethane foam dressing

PermaFoam™ is a highly absorbent foam dressing that manages exudate whilst facilitating a moist wound environment. This allows for autolytic debridement and supports the development of granulating tissue.

The dressing is a combination of two differently structured foams, an absorbent layer and an outer layer. PermaFoam™'s absorbent layer consists of a hydrophilic polyurethane foam and the outer layer consists of soft, flexible, semi permeable polyurethane foam, which is bacteria and water proof.

PermaFoam™'s capillary structure promotes rapid vertical wicking of exudate from the wound surface, minimising the risk of maceration at wound edges.

The dressing has a 90% fluid retention capacity under standard compression therapy, making it suitable for effective management of exudating lower leg ulcers of venous aetiology.

PermaFoam™ can be used for any moderately exudating wound and can remain on a wound for 3-5 days.

Indications:

- pressure ulcers
- leg ulcers
- superficial burns
- superficial abrasions

Contraindications:
- partial and full thickness burns
- PermaFoam™ comfort is contraindicated in the treatment of infected wounds as with any other semi-permeable dressing

PermaFoam™ is available in adhesive and non adhesive versions and a number of shapes.

PermaFoam™ non-adhesive will require a retention tape or bandage while PermaFoam™ Comfort has a self adhesive polyacrylate border, which is gentle on the skin.

PermaFoam™

Sterile, individually sealed, non adhesive

Code	Size	Unit
8518	10 x 10cm	3/box
8519	10 x 10cm	10/box

PermaFoam™ Comfort

Sterile, individually sealed, adhesive

8524	11 x 11cm	3/box
8525	11 x 11cm	10/box
8529	20 x 20cm	3/box

PermaFoam™ Cavity

Sterile, individually sealed

8912	10 x 10cm	3/box

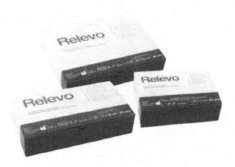

RELEVO®

The super absorbent dressing for heavily exudating wounds

Indications for use:
- chronically and heavily exudating wounds
- leg ulcers
- decubitus ulcers

Application
- apply a wound contact layer first (not always necessary)
- place appropriate sized Relevo® either side down (Relevo® should be bigger than the wound itself)
- secure with an appropriate secondary dressing and tape or bandage in place
- change when saturation or leakage has occurred

Contraindications/precautions
- wounds with minimal or nil exudate
- DO NOT cut the dressing

Product properties:
- Relevo® is made up of cellulose and super polymers, with a cover of polypropylene
- Relevo® absorbs exudates and secretions while keeping a moist environment in the wound area. The excess exudate is absorbed and binds in the dressing without leaking
- Relevo® absorbs well under compression
- the performance of Relevo® contributes to fewer dressing changes and offers a more cost effective exudate management dressing option

ZETUVIT® PLUS

An extra absorbent dressing pad for heavily exudating wounds

Zetuvit® Plus is an extension of Zetuvit®, featuring Super Absorbent Polymers (SAP) for higher absorbency. The dressing binds wound exudate rapidly and reliably, retaining it within the absorbent core.

The improved absorption and retention of fluid may reduce the frequency of dressing changes in some wounds, and offer better fluid handling capacity in difficult to manage, highly exudating wounds, such as fungating tumours and wounds associated with lymphoedema.

Indications:
- heavily exudating wounds
- primary dressing on surgical wounds

The hydrophobic outer surface of the non-woven polyamide prevents it from sticking to the wound, while the hydrophilic cellulose fibers of the inner surface create a capillary action and passes exudate rapidly into the absorbent core.

The super absorbent core contains cellulose fluff bound with a polyacrylate which helps bind and trap exudate.

Non-woven material on the backside of the dressing, prevents fluid strike-through.

On the side facing away from the wound, the product features a special water-repellent, non-woven material that is permeable to air. This side is marked in green to ensure the correct application of the dressing.

Relevo®		
Code	Size	Unit
1019	10 x 10cm	10/box
1020	10 x 10cm	50/box
1021A	10 x 20cm	10/box
1021	10 x 20cm	50/box
1022A	20 x 20cm	10/box
1022	20 x 20cm	50/box

Zetuvit® Plus		
Code	Size	Unit
1045	10 x 10cm	10/box
1044	10 x 20cm	10/box
1049	15 x 20cm	10/box
1043	20 x 25cm	10/box
1050	20 x 40cm	5/box

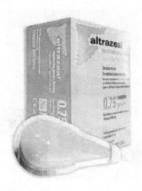

ALTRAZEAL

Altrazeal® is an advanced engineering material that is unique among all other wound dressings in terms of properties and performance. It is designed to provide an optimized wound bed environment to promote wound healing.

The first and only sterile wound dressing that transforms from a powder, to a flexible, protective, solid gel dressing in the presence of wound exudate, filling and sealing the wound. The nanoflex technology combines biocompatible, non-toxic and safe materials, including hydroxyethylmethacrylate (HEMA), that have been used extensively in contact lenses.

On exposure to wound exudate, the Altrazeal powder particles irreversibly aggregate to form a moist, flexible dressing and an ideal moist wound healing environment. This transformation occurs without a chemical reaction.

The material is non-resorbable and the pores are too small for bacteria to penetrate. The capillary forces of the dressing allow management of exudate through vapour transpiration and create a negative pressure at the wound bed.

Benefits

- Micro-contouring to the moist wound bed without bio-adhesion
- High MVTR (12L per metre squared in 24 hrs2) with low pressure at the wound-dressing interface stimulating healthy granulation tissue
- Impermeable to bacteria
- Continuous total moisture content of 68% at the wound surface
- Decreased risk of peri-wound maceration
- Flexibility with tensile strength
- Improved patient comfort with improvements in pain levels
- Secondary dressing may not be required
- Use for 7 days; can remain in place up to 30 days if exudate is present
- Reduced dressing changes and nursing intervention

altrazeal™
transforming powder dressing
nanoflex™ technology

Altrazeal™		
Code	Size	Unit
13184	0.75gm sachet (10x10cm)	Each

MEBO™ SKINCARE RANGE

MEBO™'s unique formulations are the only ointments that stimulate stem cell regeneration.

The ointments promote the natural regeneration of stem cells located at the bottom of the hair follicle. These cells are capable of producing not only the hair shaft, but also the daughter cells that create the dermis and epidermis.

The power of stem cell regeneration was recognised in 1999 by the United States "Science" Magazine, which rated stem cell research as the world's leading scientific achievement.

MEBO™ Burn Repair and MEBO™ Restore are the only ointments officially endorsed by the New Zealand Burn Support Charitable Trust Incorporated.

For the treatment of skin and diabetic ulcers, bedsores, haemorrhoids, shingles, chafed/cracked skin and other wounds.

• MEBO™ Wound Repair aids natural healing of skin

• MEBO™ Burn Repair aids natural healing of all burns, including scalds and sunburn

• MEBO™ Restore aids in returning elasticity, fading scars and blemishes

• MEBO™ Anti Itch helps to soothe the skin

Stimulating Stem Cell Regeneration

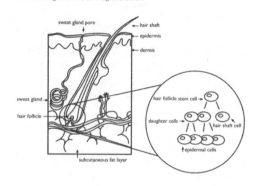

MEBO™ Skincare Range		
Code	Description	Unit
8446	MEBO™ Wound Repair	each
8445	MEBO™ Burn Repair	each
8447	MEBO™ Restore	each
8449	MEBO™ Anti Itch	each

	LATIN NAME (BOTANICAL NAME) [ENGLISH NAME]	MAIN CHEMICAL COMPOUNDS	FUNCTION (PHARMACOLOGICAL ACTIVITY)
MAIN INGREDIENT	Rhizoma coptidis (Coptis chinensis) [Gold Thread rhizome]	Berberine, Jatrorrhizine, Palmatine, Columbaine, Copstine, Worenine, Magnoflorine, Epiberine, Obacunone	Antimicrobial, antiviral, antifungal anti-inflammatory
MAIN INGREDIENT	Cortex phellodendri (Phellodendron amure) [Amure Cork-tree bark]	Berberine, Jatrorrhizine, Palmative, Phellodendrine, Conducive, Columbaine, Obaculactone	Antimicrobial, anti-inflammatory
MAIN INGREDIENT	Radix scutellariae (Scutellaria baicalensis) [Baiucal Skullcap root]	Baicalin, Baicalein, Wogonin, Campsterol, Beta sitosterol	Antimicrobial, anti-allergic, antitoxic, anti-inflammatory
CARRIER	Oleum sesami Sesamum indicum [Sesami seed oil]	Edible plant oil Nutritional protein including Oleic acid, Linoleic acid, Sitosterol tyamine, Vitamin E	Extraction solvent, antioxidant, anti-aging
BASE	Cere flava [Beeswax]		Frame structure Antioxidant Preservative

MEDIHONEY™ ANTIBACTERIAL PRODUCTS™
are topical preparations for chronic and acute wound care.

ANTIBACTERIAL WOUND GEL

It has been specifically formulated combining 80% Medihoney™ Antibacterial Honey with natural waxes and oils to provide a high viscosity gel that is easy to apply with good wash off characteristics when dressings are changed.

Medihoney™ Antibacterial Wound Gel™ is proven to be clinically effective for:

*   inhibiting bacteria at the wound bed (effective against more than 200 clinical isolates)
*   fast, effective autolytic debridement on sloughy and necrotic tissue in an antibacterial environment
*   rapidly removing malodour
*   providing a moist wound healing environment thus reducing trauma and pain at dressing change

Indications:

*   surgical wounds
*   burns
*   pressure sores
*   acute and chronic wounds
*   leg / foot ulcers
*   donor and recipient graft sites

Superior wound bed preparation

The high osmotic potential created by Medihoney™ Antibacterial Wound Gel causes a mass flow of bacteria, endotoxins and necrotic material away from the wound bed. This material is then contained in an antibacterial matrix for easy removal at dressing change.

CASE STUDY

Burns

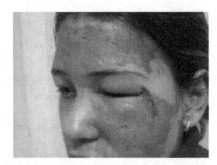

Initial wound.

After 10 days treatment with Medihoney™ Antibacterial Wound Gel™.

Medihoney™

Medihoney® Antibacterial Wound Gel

Code	Description	Unit
10786	Antibacterial Wound Gel 10g Tube	Tube

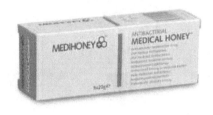

MEDIHONEY™ ANTIBACTERIAL MEDICAL HONEY

Medihoney™ Antibacterial Medical Honey contains 100% Medihoney™ Antibacterial Honey and is proven to be clinically effective for:

- inhibiting bacteria at the wound bed (effective against more than 200 clinical isolates)
- fast, effective autolytic debridement on sloughy and necrotic tissue in an antibacterial environment
- rapidly removing malodour
- providing a moist wound healing environment thus reducing trauma and pain at dressing change

Indications:

- deep wounds
- necrotic wounds
- surgical wounds
- sinus wounds
- infected wounds
- malodorous wounds
- superior wound bed preparation

The high osmotic potential created by Medihoney™ Antibacterial Medical Honey causes a mass flow of bacteria, endotoxins and necrotic material away from the wound bed. This material is then contained in an antibacterial matrix for easy removal at dressing change.

CASE STUDY
Ulcers

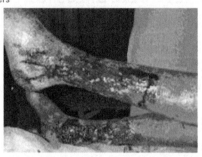

Initial: MRSA present, pain at dressing change, potential amputation.

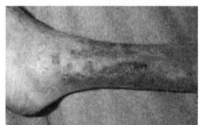

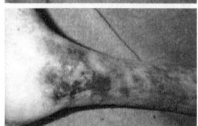

After 48 days treatment with Medihoney™ Antibacterial Medical Honey: Pain levels reduced, epithelialisation present after 1 week, significant healing after one month.

Antibacterial Medical Honey™

Code	Description	Unit
10787	Antibacterial Medical Honey 20g Tube	Tube
10791	Antibacterial Medical Honey 50g Tube	Tube

MEDIHONEY™ ANTIBACTERIAL HONEY TULLE DRESSING

- Antibacterial Leptospermum (Manuka) honey (minimum 20g)
- Non adherent

Indications:
- leg/foot ulcers
- pressure ulcers
- infected wounds
- sloughy wounds
- neucrotic wounds
- malodorous wounds
- donor and recipient graft sites
- burns
- surgical wounds
- diabetic wounds
- abrasions

Medihoney™ dressings have been shown to improve healing rates by up to 30% compared to standard dressings and to provide faster debridement than some hydrogels.

Dressings may be folded or cut with sterile scissors to the shape of the wound.

Frequency of change:

Medihoney™ Antibacterial Honey Tulle Dressing requires changing when the dressing has been diluted by wound exudate. The dressing may be left in place for up to seven days depending on wound exudate. Heavily exudating wounds require close monitoring and may require daily dressing changes.

MEDIHONEY™ ANTIBACTERIAL HONEY GEL SHEET

Medihoney™ Gel Sheet is a sterile non-adherent wound dressing comprising Medihoney™ Antibacterial Honey (80% w/w) and Sodium Alginate for wound care (20% w/w).

Medihoney™ Gel Sheet is for use on mild to moderately exudating wounds.

Contraindications:
Do not use on individuals who have had an allergic reaction to honey or sodium alginate.

Cautions

Due to the properties of honey, some patients may experience discomfort such as a stinging or drawing sensation upon application. This will subside over time. If discomfort is of an unacceptable level, remove the dressing and wash the affected area.

This product works optimally on mild to moderately exudating wounds. Dry wounds should ideally be managed with Medihoney™ Antibacterial Medical Honey™ or Medihoney™ Antibacterial Wound Gel.

To be used with caution and under close observation on heavily exudating wounds, arterial ulcers or heavy bleeds.

Not recommended for use in body cavities.

In the event of a slow or non-responding wound, the treatment regime should be reviewed.

Medihoney™

Antibacterial Honey Tulle Dressing

Code	Description	Unit
10788	Tulle Dressing 10 x 10cm	5/box

Medihoney™

Antibacterial Honey Gel Sheet

Code	Description	Unit
10789	Gel Sheet 5 x 5cm	10/box
10790	Gel Sheet 10 x 10cm	10/box

MEDIHONEY™ ANTIBACTERIAL HONEY APINATE™ DRESSING

- Antibacterial Leptospermum (Manuka) honey
- Calcium alginate fabric
- Protects delicate tissue

Indications:
- leg/foot ulcers
- pressure ulcers
- infected wounds
- sloughy wounds
- malodorous wounds
- donor and recipient graft sites
- burns
- surgical wounds
- diabetic wounds
- abrasions

Frequency of change:
The Medihoney™ Antibacterial Honey Apinate™ Dressing requires changing when the dressing has been diluted by wound exudate. The dressing may be left in place for up to seven days depending on wound exudate. If maceration of the surrounding skin occurs more frequent changing of the dressing is required.

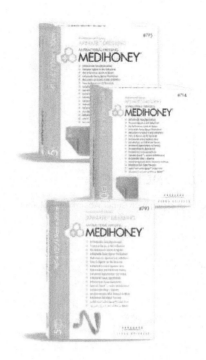

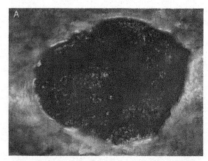

CASE STUDY
Ulcers

After 29 days, with Medihoney™ applied under a 4-layer compressive dressing. Changed weekly.

Medihoney™ Antibacterial Honey Apinate™ Dressing		
Code	Description	Unit
11973	Antibacterial Honey Apinate™ Dressing, 5x5cm	10/box
9465	Antibacterial Honey Apinate™ Dressing, 10 x 10cm	5/box
11974	Antibacterial Honey Apinate™ Dressing, 2g Rope	5/box

MEDIHONEY® HCS

Hydrogel Dressing with Super Absorbent Polymer
- Antibacterial Leptospermum (Manuka) honey
- Calcium alginate fabric
- Protects delicate tissue

Indications:
- leg/foot ulcers
- pressure ulcers
- infected wounds
- sloughy wounds
- malodorous wounds
- donor and recipient graft sites
- burns
- surgical wounds
- diabetic wounds
- abrasions

Frequency of change:
The Medihoney™ Antibacterial Honey Apinate™ Dressing requires changing when the dressing has been diluted by wound exudate. The dressing may be left in place for up to seven days depending on wound exudate. If maceration of the surrounding skin occurs more frequent changing of the dressing is required.

Medihoney™ Antibacterial Honey Hydrogel Colloidal Sheet Dressing

Code	Description	Unit
12818	Medihoney HCS Non-Adhesive Dressing 6x6cm	10/box
12819	Medihoney HCS Non-Adhesive Dressing 11x11cm	10/box
12820	Medihoney HCS Adhesive Dressing 11x11cm	10/box
12817	Medihoney HCS Adhesive Dressing 15x15cm	10/box

[Look to MEDIHONEY® as first-line of defense]

for stalled, non-progressing wounds

Non-Healing Post-Op Wound

Paul Liguori, MD and Kim Peters, RN, CWS: Case #1 of 8 presented at 2008 World Union of Wound Healing Societies

- Dehisced pectoral flap procedure
- Progress stalled under Negative Pressure Wound Therapy

MEDIHONEY™ initiated

- Rapid healing noted after initial daily applications
- Complete wound closure achieved by Week #3

 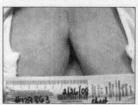

Stalled dehisced post-op wound — Week #3 after MEDIHONEY® applications

Stalled Venous Leg Ulcer

Matthew Regulski, DPM: Case #3 of 8 presented at 2008 Symposium of Advanced Wound Care

- Cerebo Vascular Incidence, friable granulation tissue, oedema, and pain
- Non-healing with compression therapy and a plain alginate dressing

MEDIHONEY™ initiated

- Compression therapy continued
- Wound heals in 28 days

Non-healing, painful leg ulcer. Week #12 under compression — Week #4 after adding MEDIHONEY® under compression

DERMA SCiENCES

MEDIHONEY WOUNDCARE AND PRODUCT SELECTION CHART

WOUND TYPE	INFECTED		BLACK, NECROTIC		YELLOW, SLOUGHY	
TREATMENT OBJECTIVE	Reduce infection and colonisation Assists wound healing Clean wound		Rehydrate Debride Wound protection		Remove slough Rehydrate Wound protection Manage exudate	
MODE OF ACTION	High osmotic potential helps clean the wound and disperse biofilms. Cleaning the wound reduces bacteria loadings, which are a source of inflammatory endotoxins. Provides an antibacterial barrier to protect the wound bed.		The osmotic action produces an outflow of body fluid helping to lift debris and remove necrotic tissue. The moist wound environment reduces the risk of eschar formation. Provides an antibacterial environment that helps protect the wound.		The high osmotic potential of Antibacterial Medihoney™ wound dressings causes a mass flow of bacteria, endotoxins and sloughy material away from the wound bed. This material is then contained in an antibacterial matrix for easy removal at dressing change.	
EXUDATE LEVEL	Heavy/ Moderate	Low/None	Heavy/ Moderate	Low/None	Heavy/ Moderate	Low/None
Medihoney™ Antibacterial Medical Honey™	✓	✓	✓	✓	✓	✓
Medihoney™ Antibacterial Wound Gel™	✓	✓	✓	✓	✓	✓
Medihoney™ Antibacterial Honey Gel Sheet	✓		✓		✓	
Medihoney™ Antibacterial Honey Alginate	✓		✓		✓	
Medihoney™ Antibacterial Honey Tulle	✓	✓	✓	✓	✓	✓

For skin protection around exudating wounds use Medihoney™ Barrier Cream

RED, GRANULATION	PINK, EPITHELIAL	CAVITY OR SINUS/FISTULA	MALODOROUS
Maintain moist wound bed Assist wound healing Wound protection Manage exudate	Maintain moist wound bed Wound protection Assist wound healing	Aid granulation Assist wound healing Wound protection	Remove malodour
Osmotic action brings fluid into the wound providing a moist wound environment to assist the granulation process Antibacterial barrier protects the wound from infection by bacteria.	Provides moist wound environment to encourage the epithelialisation process. Antibacterial barrier to protect the wound from contamination and reduces risk of colonisation.	Helps reduce oedema, pain and exudate levels and protects exposed tissue from infecting bacteria, reducing the risk of colonisation.	Inhibits the bacteria that cause odour. Helps clean the wound and lift debris to rapidly reduce odour.

Heavy/ Moderate	Low/None	Heavy/ Moderate	Low/None	Heavy/ Moderate	Low/None	Heavy/ Moderate	Low/None
✓	✓	✓	✓	✓	✓	✓	✓
✓	✓	✓	✓			✓	✓
✓		✓				✓	
✓		✓				✓	
✓	✓	✓	✓			✓	✓

NB Secondary dressings should be sufficiently absorbent to manage exudate levels

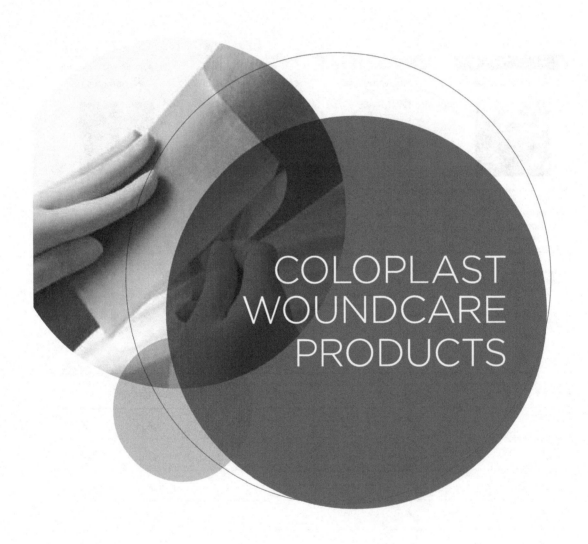

COLOPLAST
WOUNDCARE
PRODUCTS

BIATAIN FOAM DRESSINGS

Biatain Foam dressings provide superior exudate management for faster wound healing* and are soft, flexible and easy to wear. The superior absorption and retention properties of Biatain minimise the risk of leakage and maceration*. The unique 3-D structure of Biatain serves as a partial fluid lock, retaining the exudate – even under compression therapy. Wound exudate is absorbed locally with minimal lateral dispersal, thus reducing leakage, skin maceration and risk of infection, while providing an optimal moist wound healing environment for up to 7 days. When absorbing exudate, Biatain foam swells and conforms to the wound for intimate wound contact, resulting in superior absorption and a moisture balance that improves the healing process*.

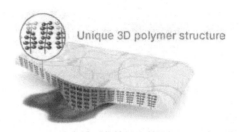

Unique 3D polymer structure

*data on file

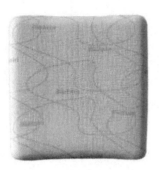

BIATAIN NON-ADHESIVE FOAM DRESSING

Biatain Non-Adhesive is a soft and flexible, easy to wear foam with bevelled edges, significantly lowering the risk of pressure marks.

Biatain is indicated for a wide range of moderate to highly exuding acute and chronic wounds such as leg ulcers, pressure ulcers, diabetic ulcers, second degree burns and donor sites.

BIATAIN ADHESIVE FOAM DRESSING

The Biatain Adhesive dressing consists of the soft absorbent polyurethane foam pad located centrally upon a larger polyurethane membrane coated with a hydrocolloid adhesive. The film backing is permeable to water vapour, but impermeable to microorganisms and water, forming an effective bacterial and waterproof dressing.

Biatain Adhesive is indicated for a wide range of moderate to highly exuding acute and chronic wounds such as leg ulcers, pressure ulcers, diabetic ulcers, second degree burns and donor sites.

Biatain Non-Adhesive Foam Dressing		
Code	Size	Unit
13276	5cm x 7cm	10/box
13277	10cm x 10cm	10/box
13278	10cm x 20cm	5/box
13279	15cm x 15cm	5/box
13280	20cm x 20cm	5/box

Biatain Adhesive Foam Dressing		
Code	Size	Unit
13281	7.5cm x 7.5cm	10/box
13282	12.5cm x 12.5cm	10/box
13283	18cm x 18cm	5/box
13285	23cm x 23cm Sacral	5/box
13284	19cm x 20cm Heel	5/box

BIATAIN SILICONE FOAM DRESSING

Silicone dressings are gentle on the skin, and easy to remove and reposition with minimal pain to the patient. Biatain Silicone provides superior absorption, fluid management, softness and flexibility. Biatatain Silicone combines the gentleness of silicone and the effectiveness of foam.

Biatain Silicone is indicated for the healing of most non-infected acute and chronic moist wounds, including leg ulcers, diabetic foot ulcers, second degree burns, donor sites, post-operative wounds, skin abrasions and pressure ulcers.

BIATAIN SOFT-HOLD FOAM DRESSING

Biatain Soft-Hold is an additional variant in the non-adherent range. Biatain Soft-Hold features a light hydrocolloid adhesive on 50% of the dressing surface to assist with keeping the dressing in place for difficult to dress areas. The light adhesive coating does not affect the absorption capabilities of the dressing.

Biatain Soft-Hold is indicated for a wide range of moderate to highly exuding acute and chronic wounds such as leg ulcers, pressure ulcers, diabetic ulcers and second degree burns.

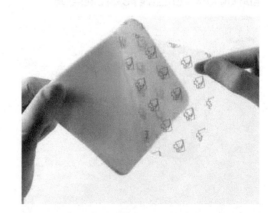

Biatain Silicone Foam Dressing

Code	Size	Unit
13287	10cm x 10cm	10/box
13289	15cm x 15cm	5/box

Biatain Soft-Hold Foam Dressing

Code	Size	Unit
13292	10cm x 10cm	5/box
13293	10cm x 20cm	5/box
13291	15cm x 15cm	5/box

BIATAIN AG NON-ADHESIVE FOAM DRESSING

In addition to the advantages of the soft and flexible non-adhesive foam, Biatain Ag dressings are prepared with hydro-activated silver ions, which work both in the foam and in the wound bed. The sustained and controlled release of silver ions ensures fast killing of all bacteria with the added benefit of effective exudate management. Biatain Ag dressings are effective for up to 7 days.

Biatain Ag is suitable for use on leg ulcers, pressure ulcers, diabetic foot ulcers, second degree burns, donor sites, post-operative wounds and skin abrasions. Biatain Ag can be used on infected or at-risk wounds.

BIATAIN AG ADHESIVE FOAM DRESSING

Biatain Ag Adhesive has a reduced thickness, softer foam and discreet design with the same absorbency as the non-adhesive version. The dressing uses a hydrocolloid product as the adhesive component, ensuring skin friendliness.

Biatain Ag dressings are prepared with hydro-activated silver ions, which work both in the foam and in the wound bed. The sustained and controlled release of silver ions ensures fast killing of all bacteria with the added benefit of effective exudate management. . Biatain Ag dressings are effective for up to 7 days.

Biatain Ag is suitable for use on leg ulcers, pressure ulcers, diabetic foot ulcers, second degree burns, donor sites, post-operative wounds and skin abrasions. Biatain Ag can be used on infected or at-risk wounds.

Biatain Ag Non-Adhesive Dressing

Code	Size	Unit
13294	5cm x 7cm	5/box
11860	10cm x 10cm	5/box
13295	15cm x 15cm	5/box
13301	5cm x 8cm Cavity	5/box
13280	20cm x 20cm	5/box

Biatain Ag Adhesive Dressing

Code	Size	Unit
13296	7.5cm x 7.5cm	5/box
13297	12.5cm x 12.5cm	5/box

Diabetic foot ulcers

Did you know that diabetic foot ulcer infections increase the risk of amputation by 155 times?[1]

The main causes of diabetic foot ulcers are
· neuropathy (often associated with reduced sensation)
· poor blood supply (ischaemia)
Up to 15% of diabetics will develop a foot ulcer at some stage in their lives
Diabetic foot ulcers are the major cause of gangrene and amputation in people with diabetes
Because of its strong association with amputation, infection control is of paramount importance in diabetic foot ulcer treatment

Treatment needs

Treat the underlying causes of a diabetic foot ulcer if possible
Use appropriate moist wound healing dressings to support the healing process
Suitable wound dressings for diabetic foot ulcers are foam dressings with superior absorption and exudate management properties
A silver-releasing foam dressing can help prevent or resolve wound infection

Tips for prevention, assessment and treatment of diabetic foot ulcers are available in: *Diabetic foot ulcers – prevention and treatment: A Coloplast quick guide.* Please contact your local Coloplast representative to get a free copy.

Dressing suggestion

Biatain® foam dressings are available in different variants to address the various needs for optimal wound management. Common to all variants is superior absorption for faster healing in combination with diverse features.

Biatain Ag – superior absorption for infected wounds

Unique 3D foam structure that conforms closely to the wound bed for superior absorption – even under pressure
Proven to help infected wounds heal faster[2-4]
Continuous broad anti-microbial effect during entire wear time[5-7]

Specific dressing suggestions

Biatain Ag Non-Adhesive
– superior absorption for infected wounds with extra fragile skin

Biatain Ag Adhesive
– superior absorption for infected wounds that need extra adhesion

Biatain Silicone Adhesive
– superior absorption for general purposes

This foot with a heavily infected ulcer was saved from amputation after ten months treatment with Biatain Ag

| Heavily infected diabetic foot ulcer before start of treatment | The ulcer after 5 weeks of treatment with Biatain Ag | After 4 months of treatment with Biatain Ag the ulcer was almost healed | The ulcer was closed after 10 months of treatment with Biatain Ag |

Superior absorption for faster healing

References: 1. Lavery et al. Diabetes Care 2006;29(6):1288–93 **2.** Rayman et al. British Journal of Nursing 2005;14(2):109–14 **3.** Jørgensen et al. International Wound Journal 2005;2(1):64–73 **4.** Münter et al. Journal of Wound Care 2006;15(5):199–206 **5.** Ip et al. Journal of Medical Microbiology 2006;55:59–63 **6.** Basterzi et al. Wounds July 2010 **7.** Buchholz. Wounds UK 2009

COMFEEL® HYDROCOLLOID DRESSINGS

COMFEEL PLUS DRESSINGS

Comfeel Plus dressings have a unique combination of alginate and hydrocolloid for superior exudate management, resulting in even fewer dressing changes and less disruption to the wound. The dressing surface is covered by a semi-permeable and elastic polyurethane film, providing a low profile and waterproof dressing. Comfeel Plus dressings are a newer generation of hydrocolloid. New technology has made it possible to develop a unique wound dressing. Optimal moisture is maintained in the wound during healing and is achieved through a unique interplay between absorption and evaporation. Optimal moisture is maintained in the wound during healing and is achieved through a unique interplay between absorption and evaporation. The superior exudate management is due to improved absorption and the intelligent semi-permeable surface film.

The intelligence consists of the film's ability to regulate the evaporation in accordance with the volume of exudate. During periods of heavy exudation, the pores of the film open widely to allow for its evaporation. This provides space for additional exudate. Conversely, during periods of light exudation, the pores contract to limit the evaporation. This gives a dressing that regulates the moisture in the wound. The moisture simplifies the clearing away of dead tissue and encourages epithelialisation. The colour guide indicates best time to change dressing and the no touch application system increases ease of use. The quadrate window pattern on the surface is a built in measuring guide, making it possible to measure the wound size on top of the dressing. Comfeel Plus Dressings are also latex free and sterile.

COMFEEL® PLUS ULCER DRESSING

Comfeel Plus Ulcer Dressings provides good exudate handling capacity, increased wear time and improved adhesion for low to moderate exuding wounds.

The improved exudate management means fewer dressing changes. This has a positive effect on the healing process and offers the patient increased freedom. Comfeel Plus Ulcer dressings are soft and flexible.

The dressing changes its colour to milky white when it absorbs wound secretions. When the white colour reaches about 1cm from the edge, it's time to change the dressing.

A dressing change can be done quickly and simply, because there is no residue left in the wound.

Comfeel Plus Ulcer Dressing is primarily indicated for the treatment of low to moderately exudating leg ulcers and pressure sores.

It may also be used for superficial burns, superficial partial-thickness burns, donor sites, post-operative wounds and skin abrasions. Hydrocolloids are not indicated for use on full thickness wounds or exposed bone or tendon.

COMFEEL® PLUS TRANSPARENT DRESSING

Comfeel Plus Transparent Dressings are thin, transparent dressings, providing good exudate management for low exuding wounds, while allowing for visual inspection of the wound. They are also soft and flexible.

The transparent dressing facilitates inspection of the wound without removing it. The healing process can therefore be monitored closely. The quadrate window pattern on the surface of the dressing makes it easy to measure the size of the wound.

The dressing can stay on up to seven days which means less wound disruption and increased patient comfort.

Comfeel Plus Transparent Dressings are used for treatment of low exudating chronic wounds and superficial acute wounds, such as pressure sores, leg ulcers, superficial burns, donor sites, traumatic wounds and post-operative wounds. The dressing is used to protect the skin in specially vulnerable areas, in the final stages of wound healing and in difficult to dress areas.

Comfeel Plus Ulcer

Code	Size	Unit
29103146	6 x 4cm	30/box
29103110	10x10cm	10/box
29103115	15 x 15cm	5/box
29103120	20 x 20cm	5/box

Comfeel Plus Transparent Dressing

Code	Size	Unit
29103530	5cm x 7cm	10/box
29103533	10cm x 10cm	10/box
29103536	9cm x 14cm	10/box
29103542	15cm x 20cm	5/box
29103548	5cm x 25cm	5/box

COMFEEL® PLUS CONTOUR DRESSING

This versatile dressing is designed for difficult to dress areas, combining a centre of Comfeel Plus Ulcer Dressing and a unique hydrocolloid framework. Offers all the benefits of the Comfeel Plus Ulcer Dressings.

COMFEEL® ULCER DRESSING

Comfeel Ulcer Dressing is a hydrocolloid dressing with high flexibility and elasticity, with bevelled edges for increased comfort.

Comfeel Ulcer dressings will help manage exudate and are suitable for use on leg ulcers, pressure sores, donor sites, superficial burns and minor injuries.

Comfeel Plus Contour Dressing

Code	Size	Unit
29103280	6cm x 8cm Heel/Sacral	5/box
29103283	9cm x 11cm	5/box

Comfeel Ulcer Dressing

Code	Size	Unit
3233	Comfeel Ulcer 6x4cm	30/box
3213	Comfeel Ulcer 10x10cm	10/box
3218	Comfeel Ulcer 15x15cm	5/box

SEASORB®
SUPERIOR
ABSORPTION

SEASORB® ALGINATE DRESSINGS

SeaSorb Soft Alginate dressings are made of a unique
combination of alginate and carboxymethylcellulose (CMC)
for superior absorption and one-piece removal. SeaSorb Soft
dressings are comfortable and soft with excellent gelling
properties, conforming to any wound size and shape. SeaSorb
dressings support wound healing capabilities by providing a
moist wound healing environment.

They have superior vertical absorption to reduce maceration
and form a cohesive soft gel ensuring easy, pain-free one-piece
removal. When SeaSorb Soft Dressing and Filler come into
contact with wound exudate, the calcium ions from the dressing
are replaced by sodium ions present in the exudate. This ion
exchange causes the dressing to form a soft, cohesive gel which
locks the exudate inside ensuring less risk of leakage or damage
to the peri-wound skin. SeaSorb Soft Alginate dressings are
sterile and latex free.

SeaSorb Soft is indicated for moderately to heavily exudating
wounds such as leg ulcers, pressure ulcers, diabetic foot ulcers,
second degree burns and donor sites. SeaSorb Soft Filler is
indicated for heavily exudating wounds, in particular, deep
cavity wounds. SeaSorb Soft Dressings should be used with a
secondary dressings.

SeaSorb Soft Alginate Dressing		
Code	Size	Unit
29103705	5cm x 5cm	30/box
29103710	10cm x 10cm	10/box
29103715	15cm x 15cm	10/box
Biatain Alginate Rope Dressing (Previously SeaSorb Rope)		
Code	Size	Unit
291037402	40cm/2g rope	6/box

PURILON® GEL

Purilon Gel is a clear gel made of natural ingredients without additives. It consists of more than 90% purified water sodium carboxymethylcellulose and calcium alginate.

Purilon Gel is used for wounds that need effective autolytic debridement of necrotic tissue thus removing this barrier from healing. It provides effective and gentle debridement, ease of use and superior rehydrating, gelling and cohesion properties without any additives. The viscous texture allows for controlled application and reduces the risk of peri-wound maceration.

Purilon Gel is indicated for dry, sloughy, necrotic wounds, as well as wounds with a mix of necrotic and granulated tissue such as leg ulcers, pressure ulcers, non-infected diabetic foot ulcers and first and second degree burns. The gel may also be used throughout the healing process to provide a moist healing environment.Purilon Gel should be used in conjunction with a secondary dressing. The gel changing interval may be up to 3 days. For removal of the gel, use saline or tap water.

Purilon Gel

Code	Size	Unit
29103900	15 grams	Each

RETENTION
AND FIXATION
DRESSINGS

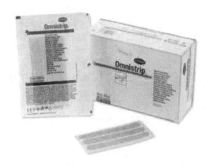

OMNIFIX® ELASTIC

The self-adhesive, polyacrylate non-woven fabric retention dressing

Omnifix® Elastic is a soft, self-adhesive fabric for secure retention of wound dressings. The hypoallergenic acrylic adhesive reduces the risk of allergic reaction.

Omnifix® Elastic is permeable to both air and water vapour, enabling large areas to be covered without the risk of maceration.

The widthways elasticity of Omnifix® Elastic allows its smooth application to joints and angular parts of the body, with no inhibition of movement.

Omnifix® Elastic covering paper has a 'wave' cut to aid in its removal from the backing paper, and a measuring grid printed on it to facilitate cutting to size.

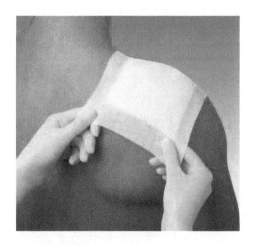

OMNISTRIP®

The adhesive wound closure strip made of non-woven, flexible fabric

Omnistrip® is a wound closure strip made of skin coloured non-woven fabric.

The low-irritant properties of Omnistrip® are enhanced by the high permeability to air and water vapour of the non-woven material.

Features include:
* flexible, non-woven material allows for expansion arising from oedema and flexion
* acrylic adhesive reduces the possibility of allergic reaction
* rounded edges help prevent roll-up
* does not absorb x-rays and may be left in place for radiological exposure

Indications:
* atraumatic closure of minor wounds and surgical incisions (healing by primary intention)
* wound support post operatively and following suture removal

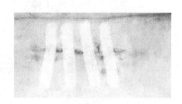

Omnifix® Elastic - Individually boxed, 10 metre length

Code	Size	Unit
1293	2.5cm	2 rolls
1297	5cm	1 roll
1298	10cm	1 roll
1300	15cm	1 roll
9423	20cm	1 roll

Omnistrip® Sterile

Code	Size	Unit	Per Box
7426	3 x 76mm	Pouch of 5	50
7423	6 x 38mm	Pouch of 6	50
7425	6 x 76mm	Pouch of 3	50
7424	6 x 101mm	Pouch of 10	50
7427	12 x 101mm	Pouch of 6	50

TEGADERM™
TRANSPARENT FILM ROLL

Tegaderm™ Roll provides maximum versatility and is the affordable choice for skin protection and waterproof cover dressings.

What is Tegaderm™ used for?

Tegaderm™ Film provides a protective cover over at-risk, including newly healed, intact skin helping to prevent skin breakdown caused by friction and body fluids.

Tegaderm™ Film is breathable, letting oxygen in and moisture vapour out, allowing the skin to function normally.

The perfect solution whenever a waterproof cover dressing is the appropriate choice.

OPSITE™ FLEXIFIX™

OpSite™ Flexifix™ is a roll of transparent adhesive film ideal for use in dressing fixation, tube fixation, dressing reinforcement and the treatment of painful peripheral neuropathy. It combines all the advantages of Opsite™ film with a unique application system, to allow easy and secure fixation of all kinds of dressings. OpSite™'s strong, flexible film also offers protection against skin breakdown due to friction and moisture.

Features:

* transparent
* conformable
* unique Opsite™ on a roll format
* many clinical applications

What is Opsite™ Flexifix™ used for?

* retention of primary dressings, eg Melolin non-adherent dressings or Allevyn™ hydrocellular hydrophilic polyurethane wound dressing
* fixation of tubing
* treatment of painful peripheral neuropathy
* skin protection under leg bags, stoma devices, etc
* reduction of shearing forces on unbroken skin, eg in pressure sore

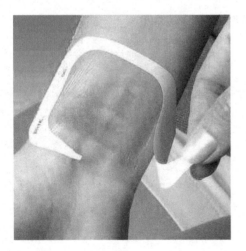

Tegaderm™ Transparent Film Roll

Code	Size	Unit
9278	10cm x 10m	roll
9377	15cm x 10m	roll
9277	5cm x 10m	roll

Opsite™ Flexifix™

Code	Size	Unit
1745	10cm x 10m	each
1750	15cm x 10m	each
1743	5cm x 10m	each

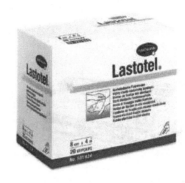

PEHA-HAFT® LATEX FREE

A latex free light cohesive bandage to reduce the risk of allergies

Peha-haft® is now available as a 100% latex, chlorine and acrylate free bandage which is gentle to the skin with significantly reduced risk of allergic reactions.Peha-haft® latex free is cohesive and is suitable for use on fragile or hairy skin as the bandage does not adhere to skin, hair or clothes. Peha-haft® is more permeable to air than conventional cohesive bandages, limiting heat accumulation and subsequent maceration from perspiration.

LASTOTEL®

The conformable dressing retention bandage

Lastotel® is a dressing retention bandage with an extensibility of approximately 140%. It does not restrict or impede blood flow or joint movement when applied correctly.

Lastotel® is 60% polyamide (warp threads). The crepe-like surface structure means the bandage is non slip and easy to apply. Complicated bandaging techniques are not required and angular parts of the body or joint can be covered without reverse turns.

Lastotel® is soft and permeable to air. It is resistant to ointments, oils, greases and perspiration.

Lastotel® can be used as a universal dressing retention bandage.

Indications:
* useful for joints and angular or round parts of the body

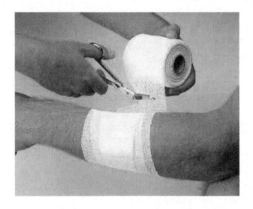

Peha-haft® Unstretched length 2m, stretched length 4m, individually wrapped

Code	Size	Unit
1346	2.5cm	each
1347	4cm	each
1348	6cm	each
1349	8cm	each
1350	10cm	each

Peha-haft® Unstretched length 10m, stretched length 20m, not individually wrapped

Code	Size	Unit
1351	6cm	each
1352	8cm	each
1353	10cm	each

Lastotel® Unstretched length 2m, stretched length 4m, individually wrapped

Code	Size	Unit
1319	4cm	each
1320	6cm	each
1321	8cm	each
1322	10cm	each
7183	12cm	each

USL PAPER TAPE

USL Paper Tape is a hypoallergenic adhesive paper tape. The tape is thin, flexible and easy to tear. Suitable for adhering first aid dressings. (Minimum buy is per box).

USL TRANSPARENT TAPE

USL Transparent Tape is an adhesive surgical tape with hypoallergenic and water repelling properties. The tape is perforated and can be torn bi-directionally.Ideal for applying around ears, or suitable for anchoring dressings. (Minimum buy is per box).

USL Paper Tape

Code	Size	Unit
9803	12mm x 9.14 m	24/box
9804	25mm x 9.14 m	12/box
9805	50mm x 9.14 m	6/box
9806	75mm x 9.14 m	4/box

USL Transparent Tape

Code	Size	Unit
9799	12mm x 9.14 m	24/box
9801	25mm x 9.14 m	12/box
9802	50mm x 9.14 m	6/box

OMNIPLAST® MEDICAL TAPE

Surgical adhesive tape made of skin-coloured textile fabric coated with synthetic rubber adhesive. Permeable to air and water vapour, adheres reliably, particularly tensile, and can be removed painlessly leaving minimal residues. Omniplast® has a water-repellent impregnation, can be left in place for x-rays; a durable temperature resistant adhesive tape.

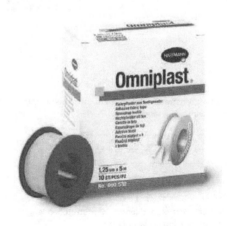

Omniplast Medical Tape

Code	Size	Unit
1289	1.25cm x 5m	roll
1294	1.25cm x 9m	5/box
1290	2.5cm x 5m	roll
1295	2.5cm x 9m	roll
8359	5cm x 5m	roll

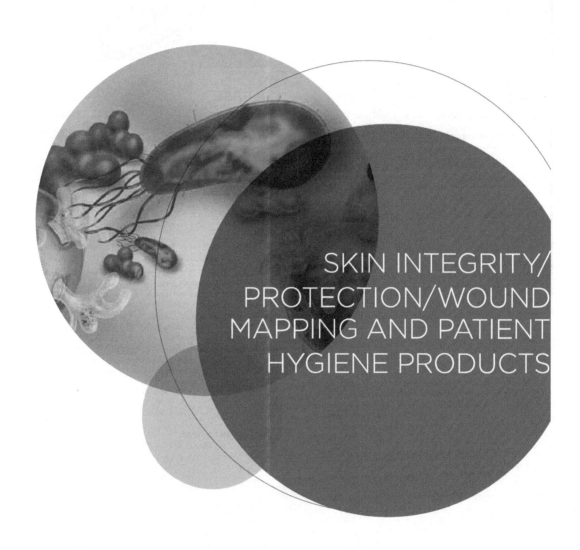

SKIN INTEGRITY/
PROTECTION/WOUND
MAPPING AND PATIENT
HYGIENE PRODUCTS

NILTAC™

For fast, painless and atraumatic removal of medical adhesives

What can you remove with Niltac™?
Woundcare - dressing and tapes: The new, proven, silicone-based technology of Niltac releases adhesive dressings and tapes in seconds. Now you can easily remove dressings without causing pain or trauma.

Stoma care - pouches: A good seal between the wafer and the skin is important to prevent leakage, so a strong adhesive is necessary. But removing the wafer can cause skin trauma and pain. Niltac™ has been carefully designed to gently release even high-tack adhesives in seconds.

Continence care: Sheaths and tube holders are held in place using strong adhesives. Even these high-tack adhesives are released quickly and painlessly with a quick spray of Niltac.

Product features
*   does not sting, even on sore skin
*   releases adhesives quickly
*   dries in seconds – no residue
*   does not affect adhesion of next appliance or dressing
*   moisturises
*   Niltac™ is hypoallergenic

To remove sticky adhesive residue
Most medical adhesives are designed to adhere to undamaged, clean skin. Gently remove sticky residues with Niltac™ wipes to prepare the skin for the next adhesive product.

*   creates a clean, fresh surface for the next appliance or dressing
*   30 large,soft wipes

SILESSE™

All-silicone protection...sometimes, your skin needs a little help

Skin is the largest organ of your body and is usually an excellent barrier. But for many people, keeping skin healthy is critical. We have used the latest in silicone-based technology to protect skin and prevent the damage and irritation caused by adhesives and body fluids.

Product features
*   protects, moisturises and soothes
*   does not sting
*   dries quickly – apply the next adhesive in seconds
*   will not cause build-up
*   Silesse™ is hypoallergenic

Stoma care – pouches: Used at every pouch change, the soothing and hypoallergenic Silesse™ formulation creates a comfortable but durable barrier between the skin and the wafer. Unlike some skin barriers, Silesse™ contains only silicones, so it will not cause any build-up on the skin surface. Feel the difference after only a few pouch changes. Continence care – sheath catheters and pads: You want the grip, but you need it to be gentle. To improve skin care and create a good seal use Silesse™ quick wipe or soft-pump spray before replacing the sheath catheter or tube holder. For pad users – the Silesse™ soft-pump spray protects quickly and will not clog the pad. Wound care – dressings and tapes: Peri-wound skin can become macerated and delicate. Silesse™ sting free skinbarrier is formulated to protect from exudate and adhesives.

50ml soft-pump spray
Silesse™ contains only silicone-based ingredients. This creates the best protection without causing build-up or bonding skin folds. So with Silesse™, you will always have a consistently high level of protection...and the spray will never clog!

*   easy-to-use soft-pump spray
*   spray will never clog
*   does not bond skin folds
*   will not cause build-up

Niltac™		
Code	Description	Unit
11149	50ml aerosol	each
11172	Wipes	30/pkt

Silesse™		
Code	Description	Unit
11174	50ml aerosol	each
11173	Wipes	30/pkt

3M™ CAVILON™ NO STING BARRIER FILM

A completely alcohol-free, sting-free liquid barrier film that dries quickly to form a breathable coating to protect damaged or intact skin from bodily fluids, adhesive trauma, friction and incontinence. Cavilon™ No Sting Barrier Film is transparent, allowing continuous visualisation and monitoring of skin at risk for breakdown. The unique formulation provides long-lasting protection. It does not transfer to, or interfere with, diapers or continence briefs possibly minimising the need to change failed briefs, linens and associated products.

- protects intact or damaged skin from bodily fluids, adhesives and friction
- long-lasting, for more comfortable and cost-effective care
- sterile, non-cytotoxic
- alcohol-free, sting-free
- hypoallergenic
- CHG compatible

Strong clinical evidence

3M sponsored the largest health economic study for incontinence dermatitis prevention and found that use of Cavilon™ No Sting Barrier Film three times weekly is as effective in preventing incontinence-associated dermatitis as products that require application after each episode of incontinence. The same study found that a skin damage prevention regimen using Cavilon™ No Sting Barrier Film three times per week had a significantly lower total cost than other product regimens.

3M™ CAVILON™ DURABLE BARRIER CREAM

A concentrated cream that provides durable, long-lasting protection from body fluids while moisturising the skin. Unique, polymer-based formula provides a breathable barrier to promote skin health in patients at risk for skin damage from incontinence. The cream vanishes into the skin, does not clog briefs or diapers, and resists wash off. Using Cavilon™ Durable Barrier Cream regularly on intact skin can help prevent breakdown caused by regular exposure to urine and stool.

- unique, polymer-based formulation
- resists wash off—eliminates need for frequent reapplication
- allows tapes and dressings to adhere
- contains Dimethicone for skin protection
- hypoallergenic
- CHG compatible
- concentrated - requires less frequent application and less product with each application
- now fragrance-free
- now available in a single-use sachet

Cavilon™ No Sting Barrier Film

Code	Description	Unit
4819	1ml Wand	25/box
4822	28ml Spray	each
4820	Wipes	25/box

Cavilon™ Durable Barrier Cream

Code	Description	Unit
8669	28g	each
2008	92g	each

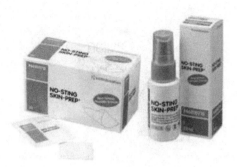 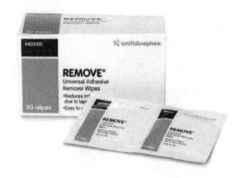

SKIN-PREP® AND NO-STING SKIN-PREP®

Protects skin and helps reduce friction during adhesive dressing removal

SKIN-PREP® and NO-STING SKIN-PREP® are liquid film-forming dressings that:

- protect damaged or intact skin against trauma due to tape removal
- protect skin from friction in high risk areas such as heels, elbows etc, that are at risk of trauma due to friction

The film-forming dressings can reduce friction (which plays a role in pressure ulcer development) from external surfaces, such as linens and mattresses, up to 75%.

SKIN-PREP® and NO-STING SKIN-PREP® can also be used to prepare skin attachment sites for drainage tubes, external catheters, surrounding ostomy sites and other adhesive tapes and dressings.

Cost effective

SKIN-PREP® and NO-STING SKIN-PREP® allow the skin to 'breathe'. The breathable barrier allows tapes and films to adhere better and assists in increasing the interval between dressing changes. It also allows for longer wear time on high risk areas of the skin that are being protected against friction damage.

No sticky residue

SKIN-PREP® and NO-STING SKIN-PREP® remove easily using skin cleanser or soap and water, so unsanitary residue is not left in or around the wound area.

Easy to use

SKIN-PREP® and NO-STING SKIN-PREP® apply easily, even on awkward areas such as elbows, knees and heels. The protective film moves naturally with patients' skin and won't crack or peel.

NO-STING SKIN-PREP® doesn't contain alcohol and won't sting damaged skin. It can be used on damaged or intact skin.

REMOVE®

Universal adhesive remover wipes

Universal adhesive remover wipes for tapes, adhesives, and hydrocolloid skin barriers.

Product features

- gentle formula
- contains aloe
- environmentally friendly

SKIN-PREP® and NO-STING SKIN-PREP®

Code	Description	Unit
6678	SKIN-PREP® Protective Wipes	50/box
10529	NO-STING SKIN-PREP® Spray	each
10530	NO-STING SKIN-PREP® Swab	50/box
10531	NO-STING SKIN-PREP® Wipes	50/box

REMOVE®

Code	Description	Unit
4012	REMOVE® Unisolve Wipes	50/box

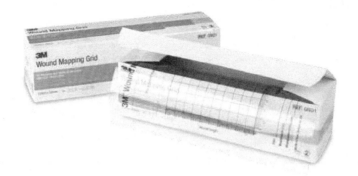

3M WOUND MAPPING GRID™

Measure and record wound size. Hygienic and simple to use.

Application Instructions

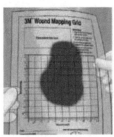

1. Place the 3M™ Wound Mapping Grid over the wound

2. Trace the wound areas on to the grid (head to toe)

3. Peel off the top layer

4. Place the top layer in the patient's notes and discard the contaminated backing sheet in the appropriate disposal unit

3M™ Wound Mapping Grid		
Code	Size	Unit
11346	10x10cm	50/box
11347	15x20cm	50/box

ORAL HYGIENE

Poor oral health and periodontal disease are known to increase the risk for respiratory infections, diabetes, stroke and cardiovascular disease; this knowledge is driving changes from 'tradition based care" to evidenced based oral hygiene in acute, long-term and home health sectors.

Colonisation of dental plaque (biofilm) in compromised patients, including those with high dependency needs and those at risk for aspiration contribute to development of pneumonia (VAP / HAP) in both intubated and non-intubated persons; studies show that poor oral care and proliferation of oral biofilm also plays a significant role in pneumonia rates among the elderly and dependent residents in long term care.

For WOC nurses' oral hygiene's relevance to wound healing and its impact on a patient's nutritional status and ability to fight infection adds to these concerns. WOCN organisations have long recognised that "oral care, in addition to promoting wound healing, reduces the risk for respiratory infections, relieves discomfort produced by inflammation of the oral mucosa; improves nutritional status, speech and outcomes for persons with wounds, ostomy or incontinence".

As the relationship between oral health, wound healing and nutritional intake is dynamic, clinical citations of note include:

"Nutrition has been recognised as a very important factor that affects wound healing. Most obvious is that malnutrition or specific nutrient deficiencies can have a profound impact on wound healing". (Guo S, DiPietro L. Factors affecting wound healing. J Dent Res. 2010 March; 89(3): 219-229.)

- The "involvement of the WOC nurse in preventative and therapeutic oral care can ensure a healthier gastrointestinal tract, improved nutritional status, and improved outcomes in caring for the person with a wound, ostomy, or incontinence. An assessment of the patient's oral cavity is necessary when managing the patient with wound, ostomy or incontinence and a suboptimal nutritional status. In addition to promoting wound healing, the provision of oral care benefits the patient by reducing risk for lower respiratory tract infection and by relieving the discomfort produced by inflammation of the oral mucosa...." (Aronovitch S. Oral Care and Its Role in WOC Nursing J WOCN, 1997; 24:79-85)

- As "poor oral health can profoundly decrease appetite and the ability to eat, which in turn may lead to poor nutrition... compromised nutritional status may result in an impaired immune response and resistance to infection, retarded wound healing, poor oral health, and, ultimately, general ill health". (Papas AS, et al. Longitudinal Relationships between Nutrition and Oral Health. Annals of the New York Academy of Sciences, 561:124-142)

- "The role of the WOC nurse focuses on persons with wound, ostomy needs, many who are undergoing cancer therapy, have multisystem organ failure, are in the terminal stages ... or are malnourished for other reasons and if they are elderly or disabled are unable to perform routine oral care; as the WOC nurse often initiates a nutritional consult they should also initiate or enquire about oral hygiene program to maximise the impact of nutritional interventions". (Aronovitch S. Oral care and its role in WOC nursing. Volume 24, Issue 2, March 1997, Pages 79-85)

"THE MOUTH IS THE MIRROR OF THE BODY, BUT OFTEN OVERLOOKED IN HEALTHCARE"

(anonymous)

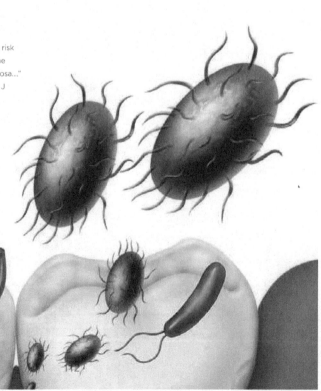

ORAL HYGIENE

Oral Hygiene and Pneumonia: the critical link
Aspiration pneumonia, which is typically caused by anaerobic organisms (commonly S. aureus, P. aeruginosa or one of the enteric species) arises from the gingival crevice and seen in both the community and institutionalised settings. Pneumonia develops when pathogens are aspirated from the oropharyngeal cavity and other sites (GI tract, sinuses) into the lower airway.

Increased risks for aspiration pneumonia occur when a sequence of periodontal disease, dental decay and poor oral hygiene is compounded by the presence of dysphagia, feeding problems and poor functional status all of which are found in vulnerable dependent persons. But modifiable risks of aspiration pneumonia do exist; these include implementation of standardised evidenced based practices (EBP) in oral hygiene, routine oral assessment, mechanical cleansing to reduce biofilm and strict adherence to aspiration precaution protocols. Consequently, an urgent need exists to improve the state of oral care for vulnerable and dependent persons, particularly those who are dentate.

Current state of oral health and care
The level of oral care provided to patients / residents is a key indicator on the quality of care that is provided in general; the appearance of dry cracked lips, coated tongue, vegetation on teeth and halitosis indicate a lack of oral care and flagrant disregard for the well-being and comfort of the dependent person. A study of 71 edentulous elderly persons in Japan assessed 'tongue coating' as a predictor or risk indicator in the development of aspiration pneumonia; the number of elderly patients developing aspiration pneumonia was larger in patients with a poor TPI score (tongue plaque index) than those with better or good TPI scores. As a result "tongue coating was associated with a number of viable salivary bacterial cells and development of aspiration pneumonia in dentate persons"*.

With aspiration pneumonia accounting for 13% to 48% of all infections in nursing homes, growing evidence supports the causal links between oral hygiene, mechanical cleansing, aspiration risks and development of pneumonia in 'high risk' patient populations. However this awareness is not new with literature going back to the 1980's documenting links between poor oral hygiene and illness. The importance of oral care as a preventative measure in maintaining systemic health has been so compelling that in 2003 the CDC and HICPAC released " Guidelines for Preventing Health Care Associated Pneumonia". This stated that healthcare facilities must "...develop and implement a comprehensive oral-hygiene program (that might include use of an antiseptic agent) for patients in acute-care settings or residents in long-term care facilities who are at risk for health-care associated pneumonia (II)*."

Unsubstantiated "Tradition-based"

Practices in Oral Care

Nursing literature abounds with support for mouth moisture, adequate salivary flow and control of plaque formation to preserve oral health but is not always adhered to; the goal of oral care is to maintain mouth cleanliness and prevent infection, moisturise the oral cavity, preserve mucosal integrity and promote healing. Mechanical and chemical debridement of the oral mucosa and teeth reduces dental plaque and mouth bacteria whilst stimulating production of saliva. Because of changes in salivary properties and production, alteration in oral flora from antibiotics, difficulties or obstacles in providing oral care, use of instruments not designed for mouth care and lack of standardised practice in oral care, critically ill or debilitated patients are at increased risk for colonisation of dental plaque aka biofilms.

Unfortunately, traditional oral care, at best, has been fragmented and creative. For patients or residents unable to perform self-care with a toothbrush, nurses and other professional or lay caregivers (such as family members) have used a myriad of creative 'implements' to provide oral care; these include Lemon-Glycerin swabs (dries out the mouth and can pit dentition), cotton tip swabs dipped in sodium bicarbonate or dentifrice, gauze sponges wrapped on forceps, tongue depressors or even wrapped around fingers, or hard edged "implements" to pry open or prop open the mouth all in the attempt to perform oral hygiene. These practices offer no true 'hygiene care" and are potentially dangerous as cotton tipped applicators leave behind small fibres that patients swallow, inhale or get trapped in the oral cavity causing bacterial seeding; and wood or hard edged implements can cause wounds to the mucosa, gums, teeth, lips and alarmingly, fingers can be bitten.

Solutions to optimising care
If the patient is dentate (has teeth), diligent oral hygiene should provide cleaning with a toothbrush in the AM and PM. Those at higher risk for pneumonia (i.e. intubated patients) or with moderate to severe 'oral dysfunction' require additional cleaning every 2-4 hours using foam oral swabs with at minimum, sodium bicarbonate to stimulate and moisturise the oral mucosa, lift debris and neutralise plaque acids. Toothbrushes are the most effective means for removing and reducing dental plaque from teeth but biofilm also clings to the oral mucosa, particularly in the 'cheeks' (buccal cavity), gums and tongue. To clean those areas use a foam oral swab (commonly referred to as a Toothette®) that contain deep "grooves or ridges" to mimic the actions of a toothbrush to clean the surface and in between the teeth and to stimulate - cleanse the oral mucosa, buccal areas, gum line, temporal-mandibular ridges, hard pallet and lips.

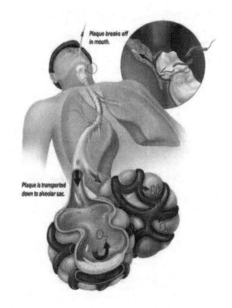

Plaque breaks off in mouth.

Plaque is transported down to alveolar sac.

ORAL HYGIENE

RECOMMENDED APPROACHES AND TOOLS

There are four components to providing evidenced based oral care:

1. Routine oral health assessment using a standardised tool, minimum of once per day and on admission; an oral dysfunction 'scoring' system is preferred over those that use only 'tick marks'
2. Oral cleansing using appropriate cleansing agents to maintain mucosal integrity and pH
3. Debridement of oral structures using appropriate implements to reduce presence of dental plaque and debris
4. Moisturising of the oral cavity and its' structures particularly in those with significant xerostomia

Mechanical debridement / brushing:

Toothbrushes:
- Use an ultra-soft, small headed or paediatric sized toothbrush or, flexible three-headed toothbrush (aka Surround® Toothbrush) for those with short tolerance due to behavioural issues as all surfaces are brushed simultaneously in a shorter period of time
- For those with high risk for aspiration during oral care, a suction toothbrush and suction oral swab is preferred

Toothbrush 'alternatives' / adjuncts to oral care:
- Foam oral swabs (aka Toothette Swabs®) to stimulate and cleanse the oral mucosa, buccal areas, gum line, temporal-mandibular ridges, tongue, hard pallet and lips
- Oral swabs don't replace toothbrushes in those who are dentate or can tolerate brushing and have no contraindications such as low platelets, oral trauma, etc.
- Oral swabs are recommended for in-between AM and PM tooth brushing and used every 2-4 hours for those with moderate to severe oral dysfunction.
- Frequent swabbing stimulates and moisturises the mucosal tissue to minimise oral dysfunction.
- Foam swabs impregnated with sodium bicarbonate avoids under or overdosing with incorrectly prepared sodium bicarbonate solutions mixed / stored at the bedside; aids in cleansing, lubricating, preventing crusting and gently removing debris between brushing.
- Foam swabs used with 1.5% hydrogen peroxide and sodium bicarb increases effectiveness of the debriding action and helps thin ropey, thickened secretions found in those with severe oral dysfunction and aids in removing oral secretions.
- Plain / non-impregnated foam oral swabs are preferable over "jumbo swabs" or gloved fingers to apply mouth gels or medications.

Lip and Mouth Moisturisers
- Only 'muco-adhesive' water-soluble mouth moisturiser for lips and oral cavity should be used.
- Petroleum based moisturisers inflame open wounds and should not be used inside the mouth, particularly for those at high risk for aspiration
- Petroleum based lip moisturisers are contradicted during oxygen therapy

Other adjuncts to oral care
- Protective mouth props (i.e. Open-Wide® Mouth Prop) to facilitate care in those who are unable to fully cooperate during oral hygiene
- Made from dense foam, provides measure of safety for both patient and caregiver reducing injuries to the teeth, mouth or gums.
- Protective mouth prop essential for safe oral care in problematic patients such as those with Alzheimer's, Dementia, strokes or spasticity issues who cannot keep their mouths fully open during oral care or might unexpectedly bite down during care.

The use of routine antibacterial mouthwashes has not been addressed in this article as differing opinions exist regarding routine use of Chlorhexidine versus other agents such as Cetylpyridium Chloride, 1.5% Hydrogen Peroxide, Thymol or GLLL. That being said, physician or dentist directed use of daily antibacterial agents should be included in patients' plan of care. Whilst the use of antibacterial's (i.e. low strength CHG gel) is advocated by many, staff must be aware that the use of any antiseptic or antibacterial agent does not preclude proper mechanical debridement of tooth surfaces.

Recommendations for Best Practice Oral Hygiene Interventions
The need for diligent and more frequent oral – dental care is greater in those with dysphagia and must play a part in any aspiration pneumonia prevention programs.

- Change from tradition based practices to evidence based practices ,
- Demand 100% compliance with daily oral care practices
- Everyone is to be trained in evidence based practice to include oral assessment, oral hygiene care and caring for dentures (dirty dentures recolonise the mouth with pathogens)
- Involve dentist, dental hygienist, oral health nurse as part of the healthcare team.

Summary
As compliance plays a large part in oral care and patient outcomes, WOC nurses should recommend products that facilitate oral cleansing and make it easier and more comfortable for patient and staff. To encourage the delivery of good oral hygiene it is essential to have all necessary tools and equipment readily at hand to foster frequent and standardised care. Using informed, reasoned choices does drive healthcare objectives and shift providers away from "tradition based" practices. Unfortunately talking about 'best practice' does not always guarantee the application and performance of best practice models. Without the development of on-going educational programs for nursing personnel and regular involvement by dental professionals, oral hygiene will continue to take a "back seat" in both acute and long-term care facilities.

SHORT TERM SWAB SYSTEM WITH PEROX-A-MINT ® SOLUTION

- 20 swabs with sodium bicarbonate
- 1 Ultra-Soft toothbrush
- 1.33 oz./9g tube of sodium bicarbonate mouthpaste
- 11.5 fl. oz./44ml Bottle of Perox-A-Mint solution
- 1.5 oz./14g tube of mouth moisturizer

TOOTHETTE ® AND TOOTHETTE ® PLUS

ORAL SWABS are alternatives in oral care when toothbrushes cannot be used. Features soft foam heads with distinct ridges that lift and remove debris and mucus, clean between teeth and safely apply debriding agents or topical oral solutions. Mimicking the mechanical actions of a toothbrush, Toothettes soft and gentle foam swabs stimulate oral tissue without injuring fragile tissue and sensitive mucosa. Toothettes are avalible plain or impregnated with SODIUM BICARBONATE to help dissolve thickened ropey saliva and deodorise the mouth.

Short term swab system with Perox-A-Mint®Solution

Code	Description
90003	Short Term Swab System

Short term swab system with Perox-A-Mint®Solution

Code	Description
10124	Untreated Toothette x 200
10125	Treated Soda-Bic Toothette x 200
90008	Open wide mouth prop each

"Effective Cleansing and Moisturizing"

MOUTH MOISTURISER

Features:

* Moisturises lips and oral tissue
* Minty flavoured
* Water based formula
* Vitamin E
* Coconut oil
* 0.5 oz tube

PEROX-A-MINT ® SOLUTION

Features:

* Oral debriding agent
* Aids in the removal of phlegm, mucus, or other secretions associated with occasional sore mouth
* Releases oxygen bubbles by the enzymatic action when peroxide comes into contact with tissues

Surround ® Toothbrush	
Code	Description
90007	Mouth Moisturiser

Surround ® Toothbrush	
Code	Description
90011	Perox-A-Mint

SURROUND ® TOOTHBRUSH

Designed for "Special Needs" elderly and orthodontic patients

Features

* Compact head with soft, end-rounded bristles for comfortable and safer brushing
* Side bristles positioned at a 45 degree angle recommended by the ADA to clean both teeth and gums
* Flexible structure and soft tactile surface makes gripping easier and helps protect oralenviroment from trauma in sudden unexpected movement during brushing.
* Covered in a non latex rubbery material with padded head and neck.
* Head and neck of brush designed to make brushing safer even with those who tend to bite down on the toothbrush

Surround ® Toothbrush	
Code	Description
90014	Surround Toothbrush

COMPRESSION
BANDAGING

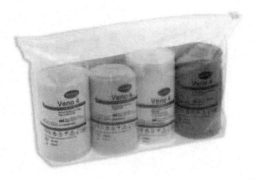

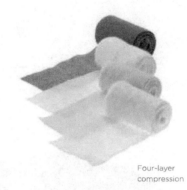

Four-layer
compression

VENO4®

The latex-free four-layer compression bandaging kit for the management of chronic venous insufficiency and related conditions

Veno4® is a latex-free four-layer compression bandage system, suitable for most patients with venous leg ulcers. When applied correctly, Veno 4 can provide compression for up to seven days.

Veno4® consists of four latex-free bandages:

- Layer 1, viscose padding bandage – absorbs exudate and redistributes pressure around the bony prominence of the ankle

- Layer 2, cotton crepe bandage – smoothes padding bandage

- Layer 3, light elastic compression bandage – conforms to leg contours. Classified as a Type 3a light compression bandage by BS 7505:7995 this will deliver 17mmHg

- Layer 4, latex free cohesive bandage – adds to the compression effect and helps to keep the bandages in place for up to seven days. A Type 3a light compression bandage. When applied at mid stretch with a 50% overlap, this bandage gives an ankle pressure of 23mmHg

All bandages are non sterile, if necessary layer 1, layer 2 and layer 3 can be sterilised in the autoclave at 121°C for 20 minutes.

Indications:
- venous leg ulcers and related conditions

Contraindications:
- should not be used on diabetic patients
- patients with known arterial disease

Four-layer Compression Bandaging System:

Layer 1: Viscous Padding Bandage

Application - Spiral technique

Overlap – 50%

Stretch – N/A

Apply the bandage without tension from the base of the toes up to the knee. If the ankle circumference is less than 18cm, apply an extra layer of padding to increase ankle circumference to 18cm.

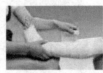

Layer 2: Cotton Crepe Bandage

Application – Foot lock then spiral

Overlap – 50%

Stretch – 50%

Bandage from the base of the toes to create a smooth surface.

Layer 3: Light Elastic Compression Bandage

Application – Foot lock then figure of eight technique

Overlap – 50%

Stretch – 50%

Bandage from base of the toes with enough tension to secure the bandage around the foot and ankle. Begin compression at the ankle using a figure of eight technique finishing just below the knee.

Layer 4: Cohesive Bandage

Application – Spiral technique

Overlap – 50%

Stretch – 50%

Apply from the base of the toes to the knee, only commencing compression once at the ankle. Apply gentle pressure to the bandage to ensure the layers bind together.

Veno4® Four layer, 18 - 25cm compression bandaging kit in polythene bag

Code	Unit
9644	Veno 4 (18 - 25cm ankles)

CASE STUDY

Irene, a 77 year old woman, presented with areas of superficial skin ulceration and oedema in both lower legs. She also has intermittent discomfort in both legs, which is generally relieved with elevation.

This case study is courtesy of Jan Rice, Manager Education & Clinical Service, Wound Foundation of Australia, Monash University, VIC.

Medical and social history
Irene has never smoked, and worked as a shopkeeper and factory floor worker until retirement. She had bilateral total knee reconstructions 10 years ago.

Over the past seven years Irene has had several venous leg ulcers, most recently one year ago. The ulcers have been treated at various times with anti-inflammatories, antibiotics and painkillers. Previous dressings included Cutifilm, Coban, Iodosorb, Melolin, Replicare, Steripaste and Bactigras.

Wound and leg profile
An area of extremely superficial skin ulceration was visible on the gaiter area of both lower legs. There was evidence of atrophy blanche and scarring from previous ulcerations. The legs had the classic inverted champagne bottle appearance.

Capillary return was normal, foot pulses good, legs warm.

Pre treatment ankle
circumference: 28cm (both legs)

Management
Atrauman* Ag was used as a protective wound contact layer and Veno4* compression bandaging was applied in order to improve venous return. The dressing of the superficial ulcer is only part of treatment: in the case of venous disease, compression bandaging is the key element in wound healing. The Veno4* compression bandage system was left in place for seven days.

One week later
Bandages remained intact; had slipped approximately 2cm from their original position.

Ankle circumference
after one week: 24cm (both legs)
Superficial skin
ulceration:90% resolved

Why Veno4*?
Most clinicians in wound care have used a four-layer bandage system with good results. The Veno4* system performed very well and the patient remained relatively comfortable during the week of sustained compression. Irene's ankle circumference was reduced after seven days, indicating efficacy in oedema management.

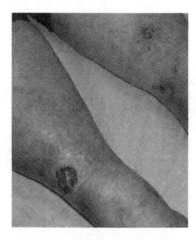

Prior to treatment ankle circumference 28cm.

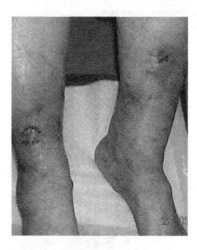

Following sustained compression with Veno4* for seven days ankle circumference reduced to 24cm.

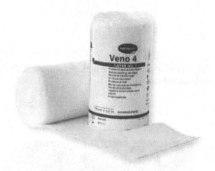
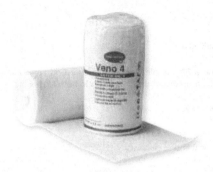

VENO 4° PADDING
- LAYER ONE

(KOB Natural Rolta Soft)
Viscose padding bandage – absorbs exudate and redistributes pressure around the bony prominence of the ankle. Made out of natural cotton so reduces sensitivity reactions. Available separately. Part of Veno 4°, 18-25cm Compression Bandaging Kit (Layer 2).

VENO 4° CREPE
- LAYER TWO

(KOB Crepe)
Cotton crepe bandage – smoothes padding bandage - very soft crepe. Available separately. Part of Veno 4°, 18-25cm Compression Bandaging Kit (Layer 2).

Veno4°Padding - Layer One

Code	Size	Unit
9652	10cm x 3.5 m	each

Veno4° Crepe - Layer Two

Code	Size	Unit
9653	10cm x 4.5 m	each

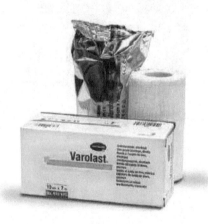

VAROLAST°

The two-way elastic zinc bandage
Varolast° is a ready to use, two-way stretch zinc elastic bandage. The two-dimensional stretch of the fabric facilitates accurate bandaging without any slitting or cutting of the bandage, even around difficult contours of the leg.

Varolast° is kind to the skin and dries quickly. The zinc paste in Varolast° contains 15% zinc oxide.

Indications:
*   decongestion and reduction of persistent oedema
*   follow up treatment after thrombosis
*   dry leg ulcers
*   support bandage in general orthopaedics and after orthopaedic surgery
*   phlebitis of deep and superficial veins

Varolast° 10cm wide x 7m

Code	Size	Unit
8374	10 m	1 bandage

LASTODUR® RANGE

The permanently elastic long-stretch bandage

Lastodur* is a wear resistant bandage that is permeable to air and kind to the skin.

This bandage is permanently elastic, durable and provides even, sustained pressure, which acts on the superficial blood vessels.

It is highly conformable and produces a very secure finished bandage.

The bandage is available in two forms – Lastodur* Strong for high compression and Lastodur* Light for lighter compression.

Lastodur* Light

* elasticity of approximately 180% tension

* compression level: 22mmHg*

* suitable as layer three in four-layer bandaging system

* 84% viscose, 11.5% polyamide, 4% polyurethane, 0.5% cotton

Contraindications:

* patients with severe arterial disease

Lastodur* Strong

* skin-coloured

* elasticity of approximately 180% tension – can be varied to provide controlled compression

* compression level: 38mmHg*

* 85% cotton, 8% polyurethane, 7% polyamide

Contraindications:

* patients with arterial disease

* fixed ankle

Lastodur* Strong with bandage clips, stretched length 7 m, individually boxed

Code	Size
9668	6cm x 7 m
9649	8cm x 7 m
9650	10cm x 7 m

Lastodur Light with bandage clips, stretched length 8.7 m, individually boxed

Code	Size
9645	10 x 8.7 m

*Bandages applied with 50% extensibility (load 10 N/cm), with 50% overlap on an ankle circumference of 25cm

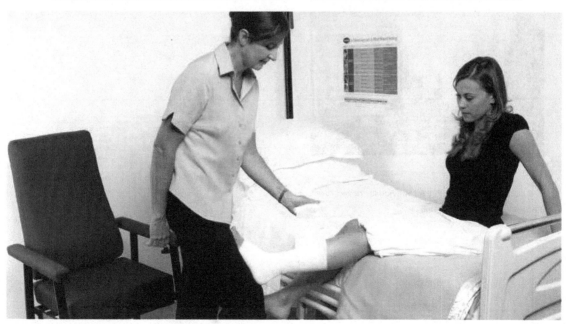

LASTOLAN®

A strong, short-stretch bandage for oedema reduction and support

Lastolan® is a short-stretch cotton crepe bandage with approximately 90% extensibility high compression. It generates a high working pressure and a low resting pressure. This allows decongestion of deep sub-fascial venous areas.

Lastolan® adapts to changes in circumference caused by oedema subsidence, so can remain in place for 1-2 days, except in the acute phase of severe oedema.

Lastolan® is made of 100% cotton and is air-permeable. It can be washed up to 25 times at temperatures up to 95°C and steam sterilised.

Lastolan® is ideal for treating conditions that require a high working pressure, including:

lymphoedema

acute and chronic venous stasis

venous leg ulcers

thrombophlebitis

post-sclerotherapy

musculoskeletal injuries

Contraindications:
* diabetic patients
* patients with known arterial disease

Lastolan® Stretched length 5 m, individually boxed

Code	Size	Unit
9671	6cm	1 bandage
9672	8cm	1 bandage
9651	10cm	1 bandage
9673	12cm	1 bandage

CASTING AND BANDAGING

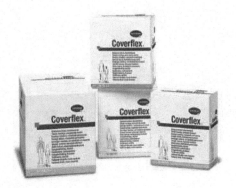

COVERFLEX®

The permanently elastic tubular bandage

Coverflex® is comfortable for the wearer and convenient for the carer. This tubular bandage is made permanently elastic by the perfect combination of 91% viscose, 5% polyamide and 4% elastane.

Coverflex® is a silk-like fabric that is easy to apply without the requirement of additional fixation. It also protects any clothing worn over the bandage because the fabric minimises strike-through.

It may be steam sterilised.

Indications:
- erythema
- papules
- irritated skin

UNI-GRIP®
TUBULAR BANDAGE

An elasticated tubular bandage. Uni-Grip® is a comfortable, effective support bandage for sprains, strains and weak joints.

Coverflex® Size 1 – 3.5cm wide for children's arms and feet			
Code	Size	Unit	Colour
7634	10 m	1 roll	Red
Size 2 – 5cm wide, for arms and children's legs			
7633	10 m	1 roll	Green
Size 3 – 7.5cm wide, for arms, calves and children's heads			
7635	10 m	1 roll	Blue
Size 4 – 10.75cm wide, for heads, and legs, children's heads and trunks			
3977	10 m	1 roll	Yellow
Size 5 – 17.5cm wide, trunks			
3978	10 m	1 roll	Orange

Uni-Grip		
Code	Size and Applications	Unit
8985	A, Infant arms, feet	box
8986	B, Sm arm, hand	box
8987	C, Sm ankle, med arms	box
8988	D, Sm knees, med ankle, lge arms	box
8989	E, Sm thighs, med knees, lge ankles	box
8990	F, Med thighs, lge knees	box
8991	G, Lge thighs	box
6001	H, Tubular form, trunk	box

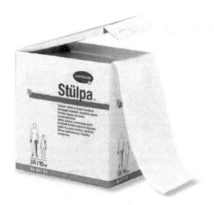

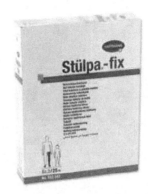

STÜLPA®

Seamless knitted tubular bandage

Stülpa® is a seamless knitted tubular bandage with high two-way stretch. Not only does it provide very secure dressing retention, it is particularly useful for lining and covering zinc paste and plaster of Paris bandages. The high elasticity makes Stülpa® bandages quick and easy to apply without additional fixation.

Stülpa® bandages fit all body parts without creasing, slipping or causing a tourniquet effect. Joint movements are not impaired.

Stülpa® bandages provide a smooth surface. This means that they do not loosen even under mechanical stress. Wounds or sensitive parts of the skin are reliably protected. Stülpa® is made of 70% viscose and 30% cotton, making it pleasant to wear, absorbent and air-permeable. It may also be sterilised. Stülpa® can be cut without fraying.

STÜLPA®-FIX

Elastic tubular net bandage

Stülpa®-fix is a soft, white, latex-free elastic net bandage knitted from cotton and polyamide yarns. This construction and the size range allows it to stretch and fit on all parts of the body.

The range of six widths makes Stülpa®-fix easy to apply and highly versatile to fit a broad range of indications.

Stülpa®-fix is available in a roll format that can be cut or slit to size without further tearing or fraying. The open net design holds dressings in position, without restricting movement. Easier to wash and change than retention bandages, it provides cool, conformable low-bulk retention.

Indications:

*   light fixation of bandages and dressings
*   dressing retention

Stülpa®			
Code		Size	Unit
15m rolls			
8378	Children's finger and toe bandages	Size 0 R	roll
8377	Finger bandages	Size 1 R	roll
8376	Arm and children's leg bandages	Size 2 R	roll
8379	Foot, leg, children's head and axilla bandages	Size 3 R	roll
8380	Head, leg and axilla bandages, face masks	Size 4 R	roll

Stülpa®-fix			
Code		Size	Unit
Stretched length 25 m			
2741	For fingers	Size 1	roll
2742	For hands, arms and feet	Size 2	roll
2743	For legs and children's head	Size 3	roll
2744	For head and children's trunk	Size 4	roll
2745	For trunk	Size 5	roll

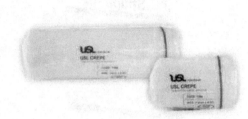

USL CREPE BANDAGE

The cotton crepe bandage for support and retention
USL crepe bandage can be used as universal dressing retention bandages.

All three bandaging techniques offer the benefits of support and relief of injuries while not inhibiting mobility.

Alternate uses include:

- light support
- sports bandaging
- securing splints
- when muscle activity is absent
- permeable to air and resistant to grease, oils, ointments and perspiration
- An economical latex free cotton crepe retention bandage made from unbleached cotton. 98% cotton and 2% elastane.

BANDAGING TECHNIQUES

The three most commonly used techniques of bandaging are spiral technique, ascending spica technique and diverging spica technique.

Spiral bandaging is the simplest of the roller bandaging techniques. While rolling the bandage, in this method, the turns are done in spiral method, wherein each turn covers the two-third part of the preceding turn. Spiral technique of bandaging is most often used on body parts with uniform circumference, such as leg or forearm.

Diverging spica or reverse spiral bandaging technique is most often used on body parts with varying circumference. Although the turns are made in spiral direction in this technique, the bandage is reversed on itself so that it stays firm on body parts with varying perimeters. Once the bandage is secured, after a few spiral binds, the bandage is rolled with the thumb being placed over the lower border of the bandage on the outer side of the limb. Eventually the bandage is reversed downwards, and after passing it over the fixed thumb it is carried to the opposite side from under the limb, and rolled in reverse spiral technique above the preceding bandage wrap.

Ascending spica or figure eight bandaging is considered to be the most useful roller bandaging technique. In this method, the bandage is alternately passed upwards and downwards over and under the

The cotton crepe bandage for support and retention

USL crepe bandage

Unstretched length 1.6 m, stretched length 4 m, individually wrapped

Code	Size	Unit
7356	5cm	roll
7355	7.5cm	roll
7357	10cm	roll
7358	15cm	roll

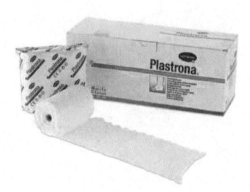

PLASTRONA®

Fast-setting plaster of Paris bandage
Plastrona® is a plaster of Paris bandage. The unique wave-like cut prevents fraying as well as cracking around the edges and improves the unrolling properties.

Plastrona® performs because it is made from a blend of quality types of plaster. It is available as a bandage, as a four-layer slab and as slab rolls for a variety of casting functions, including splints and jackets.

With an immersion time of 2-3 seconds and a setting time of approximately 5 minutes.

Plastrona®

Bandage

Code	Size	Unit
1235	6cm x 2m	5 x 2 bandages
1236	8cm x 4m	5 x 2 bandages
1237	10cm x 4m	5 x 2 bandages
1238	12cm x 4m	5 x 2 bandages
1239	15cm x 4m	5 x 2 bandages
1240	20cm x 4m	5 x 2 bandages

Plastrona®

Slab four-layer

Code	Size	Unit
1241	10cm x 20m	slab
1242	15cm x 20m	slab
1243	20cm x 20m	slab

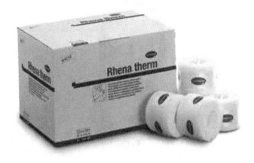
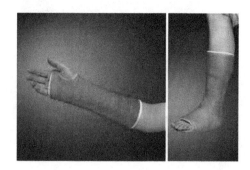

RHENA°THERM

The thermoplastic synthetic casting tape that can be applied without gloves

Rhena°therm is a thermoplastic casting tape made of a flexible textile fabric, in combination with a thermoplastic polyester polymer (free of isocyanides/polyurethane resins).

Rhena°therm casting tape is activated and transformed into a mouldable state by heat (eg in a water bath) at temperatures of 65°C plus.

The bandage is not sticky at room temperature and requires no special storage.

Indications:
* external immobilisation
* functional stabilisation of limbs
* moulding orthopaedic splints and prostheses

Rhena°therm Length 1.8 m		
Code	Size	Unit
9394	2.5cm	12 bandages
Rhena°therm Length 3.6 m		
9396	7.5cm	roll
9397	10cm	roll
9398	12.5cm	roll

SONICLEAN HEAT PAN

The Soniclean Heat Pan is specifically designed as a water heater for the activation of thermoplastic materials; it comes complete with a temperature control and digital display.

Soniclean Heat Pan	
Code	Description
9584	Soniclean Heat Pan

HYGIA CAST

Polyester Orthopaedic Casting Tape

Hygia Cast offers all the strength, rigidity and durability that you expect from a fibreglass tape, with the added advantages of being fibreglass-free.

Hygia Cast is comprised of a knitted polyester fabric which features extensible yarns which shape easily to body contours, providing superior moulding capabilities for both primary and secondary casting applications.

* strong and durable
* superior lamination
* excellent conformability
* excellent finish for smooth soft edges
* less dust than fibreglass products
* x-ray radiolucency
* excellent colour range

Hygia Cast			
Code	Size	Colour	Unit
90165	Cast Hygia Plus 2'	White Polyester	roll
90166	Cast Hygia Plus 2'	Green Polyester	roll
90167	Cast Hygia Plus 2'	Pink Polyester	roll
90168	Cast Hygia Plus 2'	Blue Polyester	roll
90169	Cast Hygia Plus 2'	Red Polyester	roll
90170	Cast Hygia Plus 2'	Yellow Polyester	roll
90171	Cast Hygia Plus 2'	Black Polyester	roll
90172	Cast Hygia Plus 2'	Purple Polyester	roll
90193	Cast Hygia Plus 2'	Rainbow Polyester	10/box
90174	Cast Hygia Plus 3'	White Polyester	roll
90175	Cast Hygia Plus 3'	Green Polyester	roll
90177	Cast Hygia Plus 3'	Blue Polyester	roll
90176	Cast Hygia Plus 3'	Pink Polyester	roll
90178	Cast Hygia Plus 3'	Red Polyester	roll
90179	Cast Hygia Plus 3'	Yellow Polyester	roll
90180	Cast Hygia Plus 3'	Black Polyester	roll
90181	Cast Hygia Plus 3'	Purple Polyester	roll
90182	Cast Hygia Plus 3'	Orange Polyester	roll
90194	Cast Hygia Plus 3'	Rainbow Polyester	10/box
90183	Cast Hygia Plus 4'	White Polyester	roll
90184	Cast Hygia Plus 4'	Green Polyester	roll
90185	Cast Hygia Plus 4'	Pink Polyester	roll
90186	Cast Hygia Plus 4'	Blue Polyester	roll
90187	Cast Hygia Plus 4'	Red Polyester	roll
90188	Cast Hygia Plus 4'	Yellow Polyester	roll
90189	Cast Hygia Plus 4'	Black Polyester	roll
90190	Cast Hygia Plus 4'	Purple Polyester	roll
90191	Cast Hygia Plus 4'	Orange Polyester	roll
90195	Cast Hygia Plus 4'	Rainbow Polyester	10/box
90192	Cast Hygia Plus 5'	White Polyester	roll

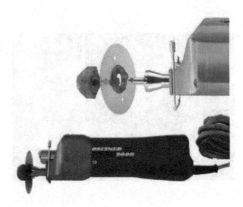

OSCIMED CAST SAWS AND EXTRACTION UNITS

The Oscimed 2000 is a very low noise level cast saw with patented anti-noise technology. The Oscimed 2000 consists of a brushless, fanless 100W-24V motor.

It has been ergonomically designed with a modern shape for single handed use. The saw has a instant blade change ability with a patented non-slip lock nut.

Oscimed technology includes saw blades with a noise-suppressing central core.

This vacuum cleaner possesses four levels of filtration (including two filters to HEPA standards) and filters dust down to 3 microns. It has a tough, powerful construction with a support for the saw and vacuum hose. The unit comes complete with an electricity supply socket for the saw. Available in 1-speed version (1000W).

- Sound level: 62dB in speed 1
- Suction: 2200mm water gauge, 50 litres/sec
- Length of vacuum hose: 3 metres
- Capacity of stainless steel tank: 20 litres
- Weight: 12 kg

Oscimed Cast Saw and Extraction Vacuum Unit

Code	Description
20101	Oscimed Cast saw
20102	Oscimed Extraction Vacuum Unit
20102B	Oscimed Blade 65mm Synthetic Blade
20102C	Oscimed Blade for POP
20102D	Oscimed Blade - Titanium
20102A	Oscimed Dust Bags 10/box
13413	Oscimed Cast Spreader

PLASTER INSTRUMENTS

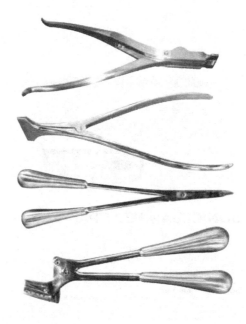

Plaster Intruments

Code	Description	Size	Unit
ID00573	Rocket Cast Shear Stille	23cm	each
825201	Rocket Cast Shear Stille	38cm	each
ID00481	Rocket Cast Spreader Daws	46cm	each
ID00480	Rocket Cast Spreader Henning	28cm	each
ID00753	Rocket Cast Spreader US Model	23cm	each
820421	Rocket Utility Scissor Pink	14cm	each
82042	Rocket Utility Scissor Black	16.5cm	each

INSTRUMENTS

INSTRUMENT KITS

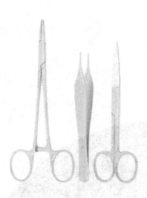  

850000 Suture Kit

Code	Description
820101	Dressing Scissor 13cm
820688	Adson Forceps 1 x 2 Toothed 13cm
822021	Mayo Hegar Needle Holder 15cm

850001 Suture Removal Kit

Code	Description
820202	Iris Scissor Straight 11.5cm
820683	Adson Forceps Plain 13cm

850002 Dressing Kit

Code	Description
820121	Sharp/Blunt Scissor 13cm
820602	Standard Dressing Forcep 14.5cm
822370	Silver Plated Probe with Eye 13cm

WOUND PROBES

Wound Probes		
Code	Description	Size
822365	Probe Jobson Horne	14cm
822366	Probe Jobson Horne	18cm
822370	Probe With Eye, Silver plated	13cm
822371	Probe With Eye, Silver Plated	15cm

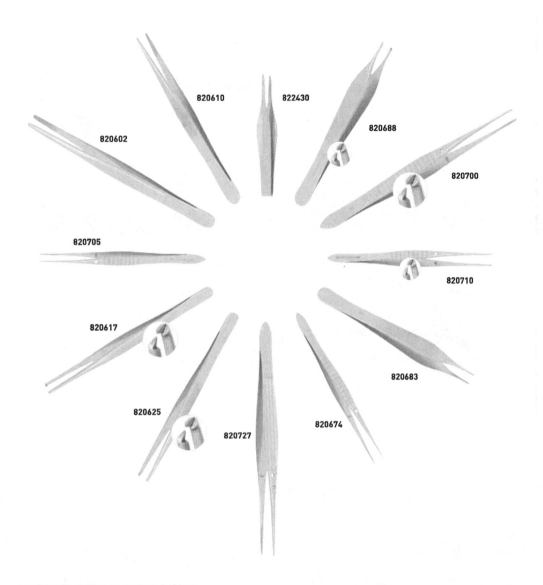

DISSECTING FORCEPS

Dissecting Forceps		
Code	Description	Size
820688	Forcep Adson 1x2 Teeth	13cm
820683	Forcep Adson Plain Jaw	13cm
820610	Forcep Continental Narrow End	13cm
820625	Forcep Continental Narrow End 1x2 Teeth	13cm
820617	Forcep Continental Standard End 1x2 Teeth	14.5cm
820602	Forcep Continental Standard End	15cm
820710	Forcep Iris Fine 1x2 Teeth	11.5cm
820705	Forcep Iris Fine Straight	11.5cm
820700	Forcep Gillies 1 x 2 Teeth	15cm
820674	Forcep Fine Point	11.5cm
820727	Forcep McIndoe	15cm
822430	Forcep Splinter Martin	7.5cm

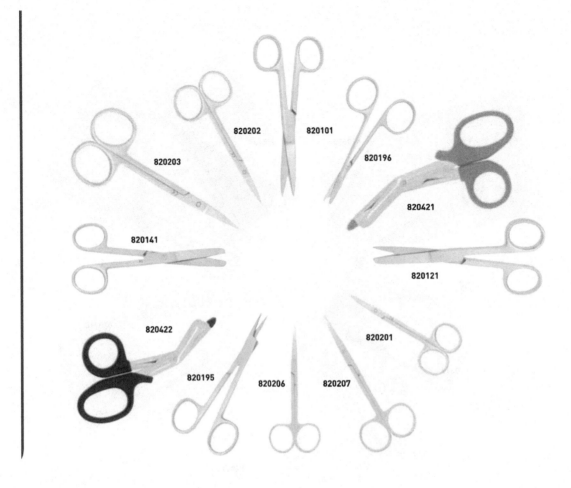

820202 820101
820203 820196
820141 820421
820121
820422 820201
820195 820206 820207

SCISSORS AND STITCH CUTTERS

Scissors

Code	Description	Size
820121	Scissor Standard Sharp/Blunt Straight	13cm
820101	Scissor Standard Sharp/Sharp Straight	13cm
820141	Scissor Standard Blunt/Blunt Straight	13cm
820201	Scissor Iris Straight	10cm
820202	Scissor Iris Straight	11.5cm
820203	Scissor Iris Straight	13cm
820206	Scissor Iris Curved	10cm
820207	Scissor Iris Curved	11.5cm
820421	Utility Scissor Pink	14cm
820422	Utility Scissor Black	16.5cm

Stitch Cutters

Code	Description	Size
820196	Scissor Stitch Cutter Spencer	9cm
820195	Scissor Stitch Cutter	11.5cm

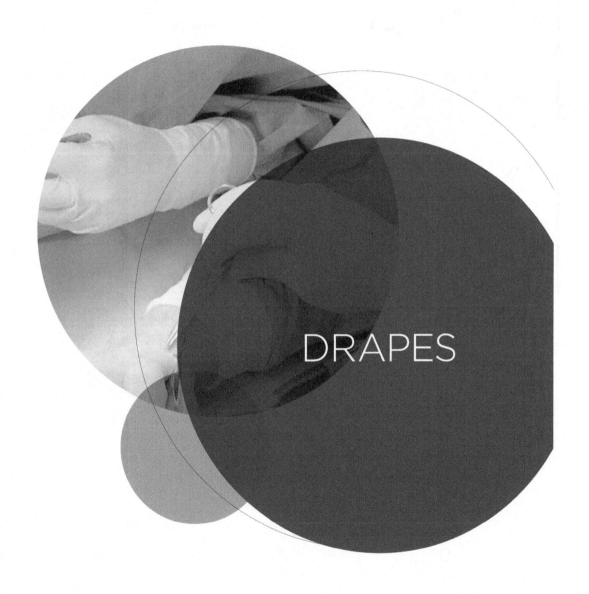

DRAPES

FOLIODRAPE®
DRAPE SHEETS

Made of soft, three-layer material; impermeable to moisture and bacteria; abrasion resistant and extremely low linting; highly conformable; also available as an adhesive drape with adhesive area for rapid and secure positioning at the incision site.

Uses

For sterile draping of the patient and equipment in the operating theatre, in the outpatient department, on the ward and in doctors' offices.

Foliodrape® surgical drapes are available in a variety of sizes to enable reliable and rapid draping of the patient and equipment.

FOLIODRAPE®
FENESTRATED DRAPES

Made of soft, three-layer material; impermeable to moisture and bacteria; abrasion resistant and extremely low linting; highly conformable; also available as an adhesive drape with adhesive area around the fenestration for rapid and secure positioning at the incision site.

Uses

For sterile draping of the patient in the operating theatre, in the outpatient department, on the ward and in doctors' offices.

Our range of Foliodrape® Fenestrated Drapes enable rapid and accurate positioning in a broad range of surgical interventions.

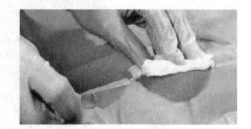

Foliodrape® Drape Sheets

Code	Description	Unit
341152	Foliodrape® Drape Sheet 50 x 50cm	90/box
341172	Foliodrape® Drape Sheet 75cm x 90cm	30/box
1303	Foliodrape® Drape Sheet Self Adhesive 75 x 90cm	30/box

Foliodrape® Drape Sheets

Code	Description	Unit
341171	Foliodrape® Fenestrated Drape 50 x60	65/box
1311	Foliodrape® 7cm Fenestrated Drape 50 x 60cm	65/box
341153	Foliodrape® Adjustable Fenestration 45 x 75cm	65/box

HUNTLEIGH
DOPPLERS AND
PULSE OXIMETERS

D900 VASCULAR DOPPLER

*Non-directional doppler

The Dopplex® D900 is a low cost audio only, non-directional doppler, principally used for ABPI measurements by community nurses and doctors in their role of leg ulcer management.

*   clear audio sounds of blood flow or fetal heart
*   enhanced battery management
*   compatible with the complete range of vascular probes. When used with EZ8 probe it is excellent for the infrequent user in locating brachial and pedal arteries
*   large carry bag and headphones included

*Probe sold separately

MD2 VASCULAR DOPPLER

*Bi-directional doppler

The Dopplex® MD2 is one of the most advanced pocket dopplers on the market. It provides the ability for high level vascular assessment, and is ideal for the detection of peripheral arterial disease. When used with the high sensitivity vascular probes it provides quality bi-directional blood flow information. It can be linked to the Dopplex® Reporter software package for high quality waveform reports or the Dopplex® Printa for single waveform recordings.

*   connects with all high sensitivity probes (2, 3, 4, 5, 8, 10 MHz)
*   provides bi-directional blood flow information and documentation
*   integral battery management
*   enhanced audio output
*   large carry bag will hold sphyg and cuffs

*Probe sold separately

D900 Vascular Doppler	
Code	Description
10044	Huntleigh Doppler Vascular D900

MD2 Vascular Doppler	
Code	Description
10215	Huntleigh Doppler Vascular MD2

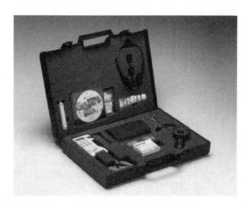

SD2 VASCULAR DOPPLER

*Bi-directional doppler

The Dopplex® SD2 provides bi-directional vascular information to the vascular professional including the display of flow direction. It is ideal for clinical specialists wishing to conduct advanced doppler studies.

- compatible with all high sensitivity vascular probes (audio only with OP2 and OP3)
- ideal for ABPI assessment
- provides bi-directional blood flow information
- enhanced stereo audio output
- large carry bag stereo
- headphones included

*Probe sold separately

DFK

Diabetic Foot Assessment Kit

The Diabetic Foot Assessment Kit provides the professional vascular or diabetes specialist with a system to help in the assessment of neuropathy, ankle brachial pressure index (ABPI) and toe brachial pressure index (TBPI).

- bi-directional doppler (MD2) and probe (VP8HS)
- Neuropen (includes 10g monofilament)
- trigger operated sphyg with a range of latex free cuffs (arm/ankle, large and small toe)
- educational DVD
- hard carry case
- set of guides (ABPI/TBPI)
- headphones
- box of Neuropen tips

SD2 Vascular Doppler	
Code	Description
ID00817	Huntleigh Doppler Vascular SD2

DFK	
Code	Description
10088	Huntleigh Diabetic Foot Assessment Kit

HUNTLEIGH DOPPLER ACCESSORIES

High sensitivity doppler probes

Based on over 20 years' experience in this field, the latest generation of the world renowned Dopplex® hand-held doppler range offers even greater performance, quality and value for money.

The range now has significantly enhanced features including:

- improved probe design with 50% greater efficiency to give increased sensitivity for easier detection of smaller vessels and calcified arteries
- an EZ8 wide beam probe for easy vessel location
- a reusable intraoperative probe for cost effective reassurance during surgery
- improved, audio performance, battery power management, carry bag design which includes space for a sphyg and cuff

EZ8 Probe: The new 8MHz high sensitivity EZ8 doppler probe incorporates Wide Beam technology to allow easy location of the vessel. It is also easier to maintain vessel contact during inflation and deflation.

VP4HS: The 4MHz high sensitivity doppler probe for detection of deep lying vessels.

VP5HS: The 5MHz high sensitivity doppler probe for oedematous limbs and deep lying vessels. The ideal probe as an adjunct to the EZ8 for ABI measurements.

VP8HS: The 8MHz high sensitivity doppler probe for easier detection of peripheral vessels and calcified arteries.

VP10HS: The 10MHz high sensitivity doppler probe for detecting smaller vessels in superficial applications.

Huntleigh Doppler Accessories	
Code	Description
10160	Huntleigh Doppler Stand
10081	Huntleigh Doppler Fetal Probe
10247	Huntleigh Doppler Probe VP4HS
10295	Huntleigh Doppler Probe VP5HS
10045	Huntleigh Doppler EZ8 Probe
10163	Huntleigh Doppler Probe VP8HS
10233	Huntleigh Doppler Probe VP10HS
10202	Huntleigh Interoperative

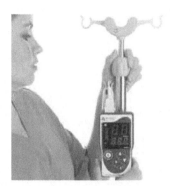

HAND HELD PULSE OXIMETER

Designed and built in the UK, this ergonomically designed hand held device displays the patient's saturation level and pulse rate on large high visibility LED displays. Fast reliable measurements can be made on all patient groups - adult, paediatric and neonates.

Key features:
- simple single key operation, ergonomically styled, fits in your hand!
- rechargeable version with desk stand >120hr operation from a single pack, automatic shut off and display adjust facility conserves battery power
- advanced battery management - tri-colour charge identification
- easy clean housing
- full function alarms - physiological and technical
- integrated protector protects the device in harsh environments
- wide range of sensors available

Supplied with a comprehensive range of standard accessories"
- protective cover
- IV pole attachment
- integral probe storage facility
- environmental carry case
- desk stand
- adult finger probe
- pediatric finger probe

The device has been designed for the widest possible user group and is ideal for either spot or continuous measurements.

POLE STAND ACCESSORY

A convenient way of holding your hand-held doppler and preventing it from disappearing into other departments.
- options for both hand-held and desktop dopplers
- provides convenient and height adjustable secure mount on mobile 5 wheel base
- oncludes basket for storing gel, probes, cuffs, etc
- option to mount Dopplex' Printa II on pole below doppler

Hand Held Pulse Oximeter

Code	Description
10366	Huntleigh Pulse Oximeter
10388	Huntleigh Pulse Oximeter Adult Probe
10386	Huntleigh Pulse Oximeter Extension Cable
10383	Huntleigh Pulse Oximeter Infant Wrap (3-15kg)
10387	Huntleigh Pulse Oximeter Paediatric Sensor (5-15kg)

Pole Stand Accessory

Code	Description
10160	Huntleigh Doppler Stand

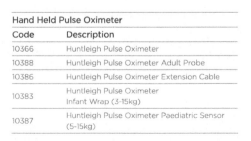

HUNTLEIGH ABILITY

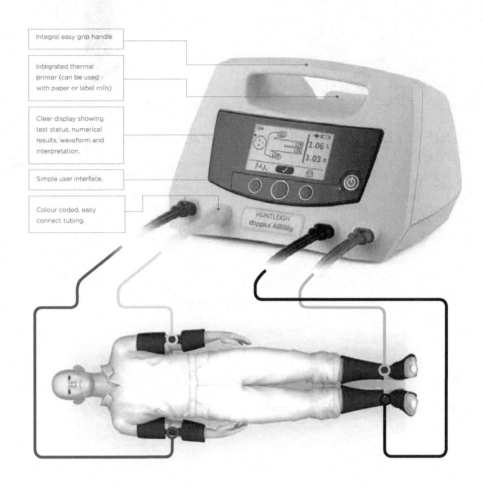

Integral easy grip handle

Integrated thermal printer (can be used with paper or label rolls)

Clear display showing test status, numerical results, waveform and interpretation.

Simple user interface.

Colour coded, easy connect tubing.

AUTOMATIC ANKLE BRACHIAL INDEX SYSTEM

Revolutionising Ankle Brachial Pressure Index Measurements

Ankle Brachial Index System has never been simpler or quicker. It's portability enables measurements to be made more efficiently in the primary care clinic, hospital or patient's home. This can lead to the prioritisation of clinical services by improving clinical pathways.

ABIs are calculated easily and accurately in three minutes without the need to rest the patient. Results are automatically calculated, interpreted and displayed with Pulse Volume waveforms on the LCD panel. The test results can be printed on either thermal paper or adhesive backed label paper via the integral printer.

Automatic Ankle Brachial Index System	
Code	Description
11296	Huntleigh Ability Unit
11298	Huntleigh Ability Carry Bag
11297	Huntleigh Ability Trolley
11302	Huntleigh Ability Fixing Plate
11301	Huntleigh Ability Label Paper
11300	Huntleigh Ability Paper
11299	Huntleigh Ability Sleeves

PRESSURE
RELIEVING
DEVICES

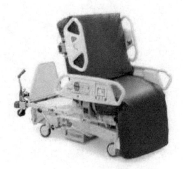

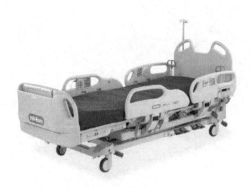

TOTAL CARE CONNECT
TC 665 - SP02RT

Features:
- air pressure relief
- heel suspension
- pulmonary-ready
- turn assist
- opti-rest
- GCI colour touch screen
- therapy statistics
- head and intermediate siderails
- headboard and footboard
- radiolucent head section
- central brake and steer on all four castors
- HandsFree' emergency CPR and Trendelenburg release mechanism
- electric Trendelenberg, non-powered hydraulic foot pump frame articulation
- Line of Site' angle indicator for head elevation and Trendelenberg
- FlexAfoot™ retractable foot control
- FullChair' for patient egress position
- cradle transition
- line manager
- TuckAway™ siderails
- Line-of-Site' angle indicators
- Point-of-Care' siderail controls
- One button Boost™ feature
- patient controls (siderail embedded)
- OneStep' siderail release
- night light
- drainage bag holders
- Wallguard' roller bumper system and roller bumper
- 6" PU castors
- audible brake off alarm
- integrated scale
- max patient weight – 227kg
- SWL 250kg
- SpO2RT surface
- low air loss CLR
- PV therapy modules available
- intellidrive – inbuilt bed mover (option)

VERSACARE BED

A.I.R.™ (active integrated response™) pressure relief system with turn assist and max inflate

Features:
- LowChair™ position
- 4-corner brake/neutral/steer pedals
- Handsfree' foot controls for head and bed height
- Tuckaway™ head and intermediate siderails with Point-of-Care' controls
- stationary height headboard
- footboard
- emergency CPR and Trendelenburg release mechanism
- FlexAfoot™ retractable foot control
- Line-of-Site' angle indicators
- patient controls back lighting
- drainage bag holders
- available battery power
- night light
- four IV sockets and an IV rod
- 5" Tente castors
- headboards and footboards available in light neutral only
- in bed scale and PPM option
- intellidrive – inbuilt bed mover (option)
- max patient weight 227kg
- SWL 227kg
- foam surface

Hill-Rom Total Care Bed	
Code	Description
11002D	Total Care Bed TC665

Hill-Rom VersaCare Bed	
Code	Description
11001	VersaCare Bed VC755

DUO II™

Fully enclosed mattress replacement system with a coated, two-way-stretch, detachable protex top cover enclosing an air therapy mattress with multiple, highly conformable air cells.

Features:

*   air mattress underlay for enhanced comfort
*   DeTeq™ sensor system
*   quiet compressor enclosed in the system
*   small compact hand control with the choice of either alternating low pressure or continuous low pressure at the touch of a button
*   instant CPR
*   instant 1 minute re-inflation
*   alarm silence
*   P-Max
*   transport mode
*   power connection

CLINACTIV™

Mattress replacement system comes complete with a user-friendly control unit, an-easy-to-connect double hose, a coated, two-way-stretch, detachable top cover enclosing an air therapy mattress with multiple, highly conformable air cells.

Features:

*   air mattress underlay for enhanced comfort
*   Vario™ advanced sensor system for automatic pressure regulation
*   AC power chord management system
*   choice of alternating low pressure or continuous low pressure module (either module can be purchased as an option therefore you have one mattress with two therapy options)
*   easy-to-connect quiet pump with pressure level display
*   intuitive controls including: PMax, Pt Egress Alarm, Control Lock out, Automatic Transport Mode, CPR Activation LED, Alarm Silence

The standard ClinActiv™ mattress replacement system is delivered with specifically designed carry bags for both the control unit and the mattress.

Hill-Rom Duo II™

Code	Description
11020D	Air Therapy Pressure Care Mattress

Hill-Rom ClinActiv™

Code	Description
11005D	Air Therapy Pressure Care Mattress

ACCUMAX™ QUANTUM™ CONVERTIBLE MATTRESS

The top of the line AccuMax™ Quantum™ Convertible is a non-powered pressure relief mattress that can be converted into a powered pressure relief mattress. Some special features include a hand-crafted co-polymer and fibre topper, designed therapeutic pressure zones, plus a gentle heel slope.

These features all provide unsurpassed patient benefits and comfort. The Convertible also includes our exclusive Airport™ connection system as standard equipment to allow quick and easy conversion to a powered system with gentle, alternating pressure capability - as easy as 1, 2, 3!

AccuMax™ Quantum™ Convertible Mattress

Code	Description
90016	Accumax QC Mattress
90120	Premium Control Unit

Made in the USA
Monee, IL
01 November 2024

69134273R00083